LILLIAN HELLMAN

Doris V. Falk

FREDERICK UNGAR PUBLISHING CO.

NEW YORK

Copyright © 1978 by Frederick Ungar Publishing Co.
Printed in the United States of America
Design by Anita Duncan

Library of Congress Cataloging in Publication Data

Falk, Doris V
  Lillian Hellman.

  Bibliography: p.
  Includes index.
  1. Hellman, Lillian, 1905–   —Criticism and inter-
pretation.   I.   Title.
PS3515.E343Z67   812′.5′2   78-4299
ISBN 0-8044-2194-3
ISBN 0-8044-6144-9 pbk.

Contents

Chronology

1905   On June 20, Lillian Hellman is born in New Orleans, Louisiana, to Max Bernard Hellman and Julia Newhouse Hellman.

1912–24   The family moves to New York and Lillian spends six months of each year in New Orleans, attending school in both cities. In 1922 to 1924, she is enrolled at New York University.

1924–32   Works as manuscript reader at Horace Liveright, Inc., publisher. Marries Arthur Kober (1925). She writes book reviews for the New York *Herald Tribune*, publicity for Broadway shows, and becomes a theatrical play reader. Her husband's work takes them to Europe and Hollywood. In Europe she writes amateurish short stories for the Paris *Comet*; goes to Germany (1929) and considers enrolling in the university at Bonn, experiences antisemitism, and returns to the U.S. and Hollywood. Becomes a reader of scenarios for Metro-Goldwyn-Mayer in Hollywood, and of play scripts for Herman Shumlin in New York. In Hollywood she meets Dashiell Hammett. She and Kober are divorced in 1932, and she begins life with Hammett.

1934   In January, Hammett's last and most famous novel, *The Thin Man*, is published and dedicated to Lillian Hellman. Her first play, *The Children's Hour*, opens in May to a long successful run and is dedicated to Hammett.

1935   Her mother dies. She writes the screenplay for
        These Three, an adaptation of *The Children's Hour*.

1936   *Days to Come* opens and closes after a brief run.

1937   Hellman travels to Europe with Dorothy Parker
        and her husband, Alan Campbell. She is to attend
        a theater festival in Moscow. After Moscow, she
        goes to Spain to witness the Spanish civil war.

1939   *The Little Foxes* is produced with great success.
        Hellman buys an estate later known as Hard-
        scrabble Farm in Pleasantville, New York.

1941   *Watch on the Rhine* is produced and wins the New
        York Drama Critics Circle Award.

1942–44 Her activities on behalf of antifascist causes, begun
        in the 1930s, continue, including publication of a
        limited edition of *Watch on the Rhine* for the bene-
        fit of the Joint Anti-Fascist Refugee Committee.
        Hammett goes in the army. Hellman negotiates to
        do films about Russia; writes *The North Star*. She
        goes to Russia as cultural emissary and visits the
        fighting front. Continues in psychoanalysis with
        Gregory Zilboorg, begun some years earlier. *The
        Searching Wind* is produced (1944).

1946   *Another Part of the Forest*, directed by Hellman
        herself, is produced.

1948   She campaigns for Henry Wallace.

1949   Helps to chair the opening dinner of the Cultural
        and Scientific Conference for World Peace. Writes
        and directs the adaptation of Emmanuel Roblès'
        play, *Montserrat*.

1951   *The Autumn Garden* is produced. Hammett is jailed
        for contempt of Congress.

1952   Appears before the House Un-American Activities
        Committee. Is released without charges, but has
        been blacklisted by Hollywood. Is compelled to
        sell the farm at Pleasantville. *The Children's Hour*
        is revived, now with political implications.

1955   Buys a summer home at Vineyard Haven, Mass.
        Edits *The Selected Letters of Anton Chekhov*.

Completes the adaptation of Anouilh's *The Lark* and writes the book for the musical, *Candide*.

1960   Her last original play to date, *Toys in the Attic*, wins the New York Drama Critics Circle Award.

1961–68 Begins a long teaching career with a seminar at Harvard. Hammett dies. Wins many honors and awards, including the Gold Medal for Drama of the American Academy of Arts and Letters and the National Institute of Arts and Letters. (Was elected to the Academy in 1963, after serving as vice-president of the National Institute in 1962.) Awards and honorary degrees from major universities begin to pour in.

1969   *An Unfinished Woman* is published and wins the National Book Award as the best book of the year in the category of Arts and Letters.

1973   *Pentimento*, the second volume of memoirs, is published and becomes a Book-of-the-Month Club selection.

1976   *Scoundrel Time* is published and stays on the best seller list for twenty-three weeks, setting off a continuing political controversy. Receives the Edward MacDowell Medal for her contribution to literature.

1977   The episode, "Julia," from *Pentimento* is made into a film which receives mixed reviews, but which keeps the persona of Lillian Hellman still before us.

I

Hellman in Her Time:
A Biographical Preface

BACKGROUNDS AND BEGINNINGS—1905–1934

Lillian Hellman is an American phenomenon. By birth she is a southerner, a Jew, and female; by profession a playwright, memoirist, essayist, and teacher; by political persuasion a liberal, and a controversial one. She is an often angry, ironic, and witty commentator on her time, and is not fond of biographers. What she wants the public to know about her life she has told in the memoirs, where, as she says, she has tried to make sense out of experience. But to do that obviously requires an imaginative interpretation of that experience; much more than a chronology of dates and facts.

For these she refers the biographer to *Who's Who in America*—but even that source, according to Hellman, cannot always be trusted. For one thing, *Who's Who* is always getting her age wrong.[1] Wrong or right, *Who's Who* and some other secondary sources indicate a certain inconsistency in this matter. Before 1967, Hellman's birth date (in *Who's Who*) is given as 1905; after that, as 1907. *Contemporary Authors* gives it as 1906. The date we shall accept here is 1905, since that was the date given by Hellman herself, in her now-famous testimony before the House Un-American Activities Committee.[2]

Many of the facts in this preface are drawn from standard reference sources: *Who's Who in America, Con-*

temporary Authors, Contemporary Playwrights, Current Biography, Twentieth Century Authors, and others. For the most recent accounts of Hellman's achievements and awards, I have relied on newspaper and magazine interviews and feature stories. The two most useful book-length sources devoted exclusively to Hellman are Richard Moody's *Lillian Hellman, Playwright* and the catalogue, with comments, of the collection of Hellman manuscripts, typescripts, and other papers at the University of Texas. (*The Lillian Hellman Collection at the University of Texas,* compiled by Manfred Triesch, Austin: The University of Texas Press, 1966).

But the primary sources of information on Lillian Hellman as a human being are her own autobiographical writings—fact or artifact—the three volumes of memoirs.

Hellman was born in New Orleans, Louisiana, the only child of Max and Julia Newhouse Hellman. Her father was born in New Orleans, into a family that had emigrated from Germany in the 1840s. Her mother had spent her childhood in Demopolis, Alabama, and the Newhouse family moved to New York City when Lillian was a child. When Max Hellman suffered business reverses (costing much of Julia's considerable dowry) he and his wife and daughter moved to New York City. His two sisters, Hannah and Jenny, who became important influences on their niece, remained in New Orleans.

From the age of six to early adulthood, Lillian lived in two separate cultures, spending half of each year in New York City, and half in New Orleans. The New York relatives were wealthy, and often condescending toward Lillian and her parents. (Hellman was to get even, later, when the Newhouses are portrayed as the Hubbards in *The Little Foxes* and *Another Part of the Forest,* and as themselves in the memoirs).

The southern interlude—when Lillian stayed with her two Hellman aunts in the boardinghouse they ran in New Orleans—that was homecoming. That was to be the remembered ambience of her childhood and growing up, and the source of lifelong emotional ties. Anchors in her life were always to be the humorous, practical likable aunts, and the much-loved Sophronia, the black woman who cared for Lillian through infancy and childhood. We meet all of these people in the memoirs, and we also see some of the unique conflicts taking place in a southern girl-child, who could be happy with a simple life in the pastoral south but felt the need to "make it" in the complex, affluent north. A southern lady, brought up to be a "lily"—but with a yen to climb trees and fish and hunt —would eventually have to reconcile femininity and aggression, in her own consciousness as well as in the public image. Even now, when Hellman is in her seventies, the image she projects is both ladylike and tough: clothes-conscious to the point of occasional vanity; "difficult" to the point of occasional ferocity.

To be Jewish in the old south posed another problem of identity, especially if the family were an old one and not orthodox. Many young southern Jews were not aware of semitism—pro or anti—during their childhood. And when they became aware, they realized very slowly, and sometimes painfully, that their self-concepts as Americans, or Louisianians, or New Yorkers, were not the whole story. Whether they liked it or not, the rest of the world thought of them as an ethnic, not a religious, group. This identity came home to many for the first time during the Hitler holocaust. Hellman, in *Scoundrel Time*, remarks that her own awareness of antisemitism dated from a visit to Bonn, Germany, where she intended to enroll at the university: "Then for the first time in my life I thought about being a Jew." She was twenty-four.

Hellman's formal education in grammar school and high school was split, as were her living arrangements, between New Orleans and New York. The widely differing standards and the broken-up semesters made schooling a matter of boredom in the south and fear of failure in

the north. From 1922 through 1924, she attended New
York University, but that milieu was not hers, even
though she remembers being introduced to the philos-
ophies of Kant, Hegel, Marx, and Engels. Later she took
courses at Columbia and was deeply impressed by read-
ings in Dostoevsky, Dante, Melville, and even Lewis
Carroll. But on the whole, the university approach to
writing and to literature was not for Hellman—not until
about forty years later when she herself became a member of the academic establishment. At eighteen, as a
junior, she left college. At nineteen she had her first job,
reading manuscripts for the publishing house of Horace
Liveright.

This was an exciting introduction to the literary mar-
ketplace, and may have set the direction of Hellman's
future more than she knew. In *An Unfinished Woman* she
emphasized the "party" atmosphere at the publishers'
(although even that had serious overtones). But as she
said, "A job with any publishing house was a plum, but
a job with Horace Liveright was a bag of plums." Among
the writers "they discovered, or persuaded over . . ." were
"Faulkner, Freud, Hemingway, O'Neill, Hart Crane,
Sherwood Anderson, Dreiser, E. E. Cummings, and many
other less talented but remarkable people. . . ."

But Hellman remembers this as a period of social
and sexual, rather than literary, exploration. She went to
the constant parties, was as casual about sex as most of
her generation, had an abortion and then in 1925 married
the man who was responsible for her pregnancy, Arthur
Kober. Kober at that time was a theatrical press agent,
but was later to become a successful and popular writer
and humorist, author of some thirty films, and two long-
running Broadway shows, *Having a Wonderful Time*
(1937) and *Wish You Were Here* (1952).

During the years of her marriage, Hellman played at
being a housewife, a part-time student, and European

tourist, but was always casting around for something constructive to do. She wrote what she calls a couple of "lady-writer" stories, which were published in *The Paris Comet*, a magazine for which Kober worked. For a time she wrote theatrical publicity and book reviews, reading plays for a group that was eventually to be headed by Herman Shumlin, later the producer of her own first five plays. She even demonstrated her sense of what would go in the theater by spotting the manuscript of Shumlin's spectacular long-run play, later to be a movie, "Grand Hotel."

But Hellman's future really began to take shape in 1929 after the trip to Germany when she became aware of antisemitism, and when, upon her return, she and Kober moved to Hollywood. There she read and wrote reports on manuscripts for Metro-Goldwyn-Mayer. The job was drudgery. She detested the shoddy Hollywood setting and the long terrifying drives in throughway traffic—but she was gaining skills and making contacts that were to last a lifetime. The links were close between Hollywood and Broadway; in those pretelevision days, the film industry was hungry for material, and some of our best writers and playwrights also worked in Hollywood. Hellman met many of them. Her closest friends at that time were the humorist, S. J. Perelman, and his wife; the novelist, Nathanael West (Mrs. Perelman's brother); and the writer of detective fiction—and former Pinkerton detective—Dashiell Hammett.

Lillian Hellman and Hammett—known to her and their friends as Dash—were to live together (on and off) for the next thirty-one years. Her marriage to Arthur Kober had long been deteriorating, and ended with an amicable divorce in 1932. Hammett was thirteen years older than Hellman, a successful writer and film scenarist, the possessor of a quiet, ironic sense of humor and an idealistic commitment to political radicalism. He was to become her home base—friend, companion, critic, disciplinarian, mentor—even in the times when he suffered from alcoholism, illness, and neurosis.

Hammett was at this time hard at work on what was to be his best-known book—and later film—*The Thin Man*. The character of Nora Charles in that book was modeled on Lillian Hellman. She, in turn, began to understand the difficult demands of professional writing, and set to work in earnest. She published two "short-short stories" in the *American Spectator* (September, 1933; January, 1934). She also collaborated with Louis Kronenberger on a farce called *The Dear Queen* (copyrighted in 1932), which almost, but—mercifully—not quite, reached the stage in 1934.

More importantly, she had begun work, with Hammett's encouragement and criticism, on her first serious play, *The Children's Hour*. Herman Shumlin, her friend and former boss, read the play and decided to produce it, even before he had finished the first reading. The play was an immediate and long-running hit.

In the 1930s the plot of *The Children's Hour* made it a succès de scandale: two young headmistresses of a girls' school are accused by a vindictive schoolgirl of having a lesbian relationship. The rumor results in the social ruin of both teachers and, ultimately, the suicide of one. In 1952, the play was successfully revived; then it spoke to the audience about the events of those times— the ruin of careers and lives by the "McCarthy" technique of the smear, the blacklist, and the "big lie." But between the two productions of *The Children's Hour*, the tumult of world events had changed more meanings than just those of this play. The world had seen the rise of Hitler, the Nazi holocaust, and World War II; the founding of the state of Israel; the increasing power of Russia and communism, and, in the 1950s, the Korean "military action." History, and the commitments of her friends, were to turn Hellman into a political as well as a literary figure, whether she wanted it that way or not.

In the early 1930s the world had already divided into ideological and political camps, rumbling toward world conflict. American attitudes toward communism were confused by the facts of American allegiance: the Russian revolution of 1917 had been followed, eventually, by American recognition of the Soviet Union in 1934; then, with the Nazi-Soviet pact in 1939, Russia had become a villain and potential enemy; a few years later she was to be our heroic ally in World War II. Concern with the great depression and unemployment, as well as fears of involvement in another war, kept most Americans from acknowledging the threat of events in Germany, Spain, and Italy. Lillian Hellman had been made aware of that threat in 1929 in Germany. On subsequent trips to Europe, especially those in 1934 and 1937, she was to know first-hand the destruction of human life and freedom left in the wake of fascism.

She tells the story in *An Unfinished Woman* and in the "Julia" chapter of *Pentimento*. I do not know how literally we can take the story of "Julia" as biography, but certainly its outlines must be factual.* The protagonist was Lillian's close friend in childhood and youth. She was the daughter of a wealthy American family, and, according to the memoir, studied in Europe, first at Oxford and later as a student of Freud's in Vienna. By 1934, Julia had become a socialist, active in the anti-Nazi underground. While Hellman was in Europe that year, Julia

---

* Miss Hellman is so determined to keep the identity of the real Julia a secret, that she creates deliberate confusion for the reader between the characters of "Alice," "Marie-Louise," and "Marie-Louise's" brother, "Hal," in *An Unfinished Woman* and those of "Julia," "Anne-Marie," and *her* brother, "Sammy," in *Pentimento*.

was badly injured in the Floridsdorf battle between socialist workers and Austrian troops and cooperating Nazis. Hellman visited her in the hospital in Vienna, tried to help, but Julia disappeared. None of Hellman's efforts to find her friend succeeded, and she returned to the United States. The following year, Hellman heard from Julia and learned that she was still active in the anti-Nazi underground.

Two years later, in 1937, Hellman planned another European tour, using as an excuse an invitation to attend a theater festival in Moscow. The itinerary was indefinite, until she talked on the telephone from Paris to Julia in Vienna. The upshot of that conversation was that Hellman found herself smuggling $50,000 from Paris, across the German border, into Berlin. In Berlin, Hellman was to change trains and proceed to Moscow—always with the danger of being found out by the Nazis. With the help of a carefully contrived escort system, she completed the mission. In the short period between trains she was taken to Julia in Berlin. As Hellman feared, Julia had been mutilated—had lost a leg—in the 1934 Austrian Civil War. The money Hellman had carried was Julia's, and was to be used for the relief of both Jewish and non-Jewish antifascists.

Shaken by the Berlin encounter, Hellman went on to Moscow, only to discover later that she had narrowly escaped arrest. Her trunk arrived two weeks late, thoroughly ransacked. She could not know then that a year later Julia was to be murdered by the Nazis, and that only Hellman would care enough to bring the body home for cremation, unclaimed by Julia's family.

It is no wonder that after the Berlin episode Hellman found the 1937 Moscow theater festival a bore and her meetings at that time with Russian officialdom inconsequential. (She did not even know that this was the time of one of the most severe of the Soviet purges.) She returned to Paris and there made the decision to go to Spain.

The republican government of Spain had been established in 1931, following the overthrow of the dictator, Primo de Rivera, and the exile of King Alphonso XIII. The Republic was controlled by a coalition of many factions, largely leftist, and these initiated social reforms designed to improve the conditions of the poor. In 1936, Spain was invaded by a reactionary rebel force soon to be under the leadership of General Francisco Franco. This army represented the interests of the military, high clergy, land-owning aristocracy, and big industry. Franco's purpose was to overthrow the legally constituted Republic, and to establish a dictatorship on the Fascist model.

The only major-power support for the Republic came from Soviet Russia, and that was largely token. (Stalin did not consider the communist factions in Spain useful to his own purposes). The democracies could not, because of noninterventionist policies, come officially to the aid of the Republic, although Franco was receiving aid from Germany and Italy. To many Americans and citizens of other democracies, the Spanish Republic seemed to represent the last hope for individual liberty in Europe, and the lineup of forces in that war became symbolic. The choice to support the republic had to be made, regardless of the imperfections and confusions of the Spanish republicans, and regardless of their support by many various communist ideologies. As it turned out, none of these was unified or strong enough to overcome Franco's forces, and in 1939, when Russia withdrew its support, the republic fell.

It was the European and American communists and socialists who organized the military resistance to Franco in the form of the International Brigade and the Abraham Lincoln Brigade. While the brigades originated with the Comintern, the members were not all communists, or

even socialists. Many were believers in Jeffersonian democracy, in the opposition to tyranny; all felt angry,
guilty, and frustrated that their own governments were,
in effect, appeasing the fascist powers. As Hellman said,
"Never before, and never since, in my lifetime, were
liberals, radicals, intellectuals, and educated middle-class
to come together in single, forceful alliance."

Hellman's trip to Spain in 1937 had not been really
planned—but then it was not entirely unpremeditated
either. Earlier that same year she had agreed to make a
documentary film about Spain with Archibald MacLeish,
Ernest Hemingway, and the film director Joris Ivens.
Because of illness she had been unable to complete the
assignment, and Hemingway and Ivens had produced,
without her, the very moving film entitled *The Spanish
Earth*.

So, in Paris in 1937 when, at dinner, Otto Simon
suggested that she should go to Spain, Hellman readily
agreed. Simon was a communist, author of *The Brown
Book of the Hitler Terror*, and at this time, according to
Hellman, "a kind of press chief for the Spanish Republican Government." (He had been born in Prague, fled the
Nazis, and was finally executed by them in Prague.) As
Hellman wrote, "It didn't take much persuasion [for her
to go to Spain]: I had strong convictions about the Spanish War, about Fascism-Nazism, strong enough to push
just below the surface my fear of the danger of war."

She encountered that danger first in Valencia that
October when the city was under fire by both sides. She
went through air raids; saw the damage done by Italian
bombs. She scrambled over the rubble and witnessed the
suffering of the victims. She visited the hospital of the
International Brigade in Benicasin—escorted by Gustav
Regler, a well-known anti-Nazi German novelist, who had
become a leader of the Brigade. There was not much
Hellman could do in Valencia except to record her im-
pressions and her admiration for the soldiers in the Bri-

gade, whom she described as "noble"—a word not easy
for her to use. In Madrid, in the company of Hemingway
and other involved foreigners, Hellman was able to take
a more active part in the struggle. She made speeches to
the International Brigade, did recordings to be translated,
made a radio broadcast to Paris, and visited hospitals and
a nursery.

In *An Unfinished Woman*, Hellman describes the
aftermath of that 1937 journey as "the root-time of my
turning toward the radical movements of the late thirties."
Then she adds that she was late, and was never completely committed. But for her, as for many liberals who
turned toward radicalism because there seemed no place
else to turn, the consequences in later life were to be
serious.

The years between the brief Russian visit of 1937 and
the second "mission to Moscow" in 1944, were taken up
largely with playwriting, but saw also some participation
in liberal activism—which Hellman is inclined to dismiss
in the memoirs as "idle lady stuff . . . speeches at rallies
for this or that, bundles for something or other. . . ." Her
growing political education consisted of reading leftist
philosophers with Hammett who was, of course, dedicated
to his own version of Marxism and was probably a communist party member.

In 1936, Hellman had written an unsuccessful play
about unions and strikebreaking, *Days to Come*. Although
Hellman said the play was not intended to portray the
class struggle, but rather that between individuals, audiences saw it as highly political. Then came *The Little
Foxes* produced in 1939, *Watch on the Rhine* in 1941;
a film about Russia, *The North Star*, in 1943, and *The
Searching Wind* in 1944.

The Little Foxes drew on Hellman's knowledge of the
American south and her own family. *Watch on the Rhine*
and *The Searching Wind* were both concerned with the
struggle against fascism and the response (or lack of it)

of middle-class Americans to the issues of World War II. The sentiments of *The North Star* and the last two plays were obvious. But even *The Little Foxes*, with its attack on exploitive southern merchants and class speculation, earned its author the label of "leftwinger" or "fellow-traveler" among conservatives, to whom antifascist (especially if not spelled out as anti-Nazi) meant pro-communist.

Most of Hellman's prewar "bundles for something or other" activities were connected with organizations or causes also tarred with the red brush. She had solicited contributions to the Emergency Anti-Fascist Refugee Fund and had allowed the Joint Anti-Fascist Refugee Committee (destined to be high on McCarthy's list of communist-front organizations) to publish for its benefit an expensive limited edition of *Watch on the Rhine*, with a dedication by Hellman's long-time friend, Dorothy Parker, herself active in antifascist causes.

There was also a much-aired battle with Tallulah Bankhead, then playing Regina in *The Little Foxes*. Apparently Bankhead had refused to do a benefit performance for Spanish refugees at Hellman's request, and Hellman refused to do one for Finnish refugees from Russia at Bankhead's request. Hellman felt that Finland was actually pro-Nazi. There are several conflicting versions of this row, but the upshot for Hellman was that she was again labeled as procommunist.

America had gone to war in December 1941. In 1942, Hammett enlisted, and Hellman felt that she must participate more actively in the war. Early in 1942 she had agreed to do a documentary film, with William Wyler, about the war in Russia, but the project never matured. She did begin work, however, on the semidocumentary, *The North Star*, but, after much rewriting by the director, Lewis Milestone, the film had become such Hollywood hokum that Hellman bought back her Goldwyn contract.[3] One version, presumably Hellman's original, has been pub-

lished under her name, however, with an introduction by
Louis Kronenberger and an "author's note" by Hellman
explaining the cinematic terminology.[4] Serious critics,
American and Russian, did not think much of *The North
Star*, but Russian audiences liked it. That may have been
one reason that Hellman (with the approval of both
Moscow and Washington) was invited on a cultural-
exchange mission to Russia in 1944. The diaries of that
visit formed the basis of a magazine article, and later,
of important chapters in *An Unfinished Woman*.

On her return to the United States, Miss Hellman
continued the activities which were to lead to the events
of spring 1952. With her usual genius for espousing the
most conspicuous of liberal causes, she joined, in 1946,
the Independent Citizen's Committee for the Arts, Sciences, and Professions, known also as ICCASP, or ICC
for short. This was truly a "star-studded" organization,
including such illustrious representatives of their various
fields as Einstein and Oppenheimer, Orson Welles and
Frank Sinatra. But, as one writer described it, ICC was
also "the major political arm of the Russophile left."[5]

Along with other liberal political action committees,
the ICC placed its hopes for important reforms (full employment, minimum wage, friendship with Russia, aboli-
tion of HUAC, etc.) in a third party which could operate
outside the platforms of the Republicans or Democrats.
The strongest candidate for President seemed to be
Henry A. Wallace, one-time Secretary of Agriculture and
Vice President under Roosevelt, and Secretary of Com-
merce under Truman. Wallace was running on the ticket of
the Progressive Party. Hellman campaigned for him in
1948, but in *Scoundrel Time*, describes the doubts she
soon developed about his qualifications. Publicly at the
time, however, she gave Wallace her strongest support,
even praising him to Marshal Tito of Yugoslavia.

For in October of that same election year Hellman
accepted a writing assignment for the New York *Star*

(successor to *PM*) that took her to Prague, Belgrade, and Paris. Her prime goal was the interview with Tito, but she was warmly greeted by both high officials and ordinary people in Czechoslovakia as well as Yugoslavia. In her articles in the *Star* she pleaded for tolerance and understanding of the Communists on the part of the western nations. As was to be her custom, Hellman based her political convictions on her intuition and personal experience. The Communists whom she had met had always been nice to her, and she returned the compliment.

Between writing her adaptation of *Montserrat* (a historical drama by the French playwright Roblès) and running her farm in Pleasantville, New York, Hellman helped to chair a stormy dinner at the Waldorf hotel marking the opening of the Cultural and Scientific Conference for World Peace, sponsored by the National Council of the Arts, Sciences and Professions. (This was an offshoot of, or successor to, the ICC; many of the participants belonged to that organization.) The storm over the conference had been rising ever since its inception, and since the first Russian delegation—appointed by the Soviet government—had accepted their invitations. The state department (along with hundreds of well-known intellectuals who withdrew from or questioned the conference) was convinced that the conference table would be used as a sounding board for Soviet propaganda. At one time the state department alleged that some of the delegates were members of the Russian secret police— an allegation strongly denied. The department refused to grant visas to delegates from France, Italy, Rumania, and Hungary, and to three of the four Britons invited, on the grounds that these were not official representatives of their countries.

When one looks at the information available to the public at this time, it is no wonder that such animosity should have been turned upon a "world peace" conference. This came not only from some liberal intellectuals who refused to attend or who challenged delegates on the floor. Five thousand people planned to picket (2,000 were permitted by police). The pickets included paraplegic veterans in wheelchairs, Gold Star Mothers and other kneeling and praying women, and even members of the musicians' union, who had invited the Russian composer, Shostakovich, to defect and join them. The confusion, disillusion, and panic are predictable when one reads even the most respectable newspapers and popular news magazines of March 1949—the month of the conference.

The last signers were just joining NATO, the North Atlantic Treaty Organization, which was under fire by the Russians, including those at the Waldorf conference. Russia had been withdrawing personnel from the United Nations, and there were fears in all quarters that the cold war might become hot. Spies seemed to be everywhere. Just two weeks before the conference, Judith Coplon had been arrested in the act of handing documents to a Russian spy. On March 2, the American Communist Party had announced that in case of war with the Soviet Union, the party would not support the United States, and, at the very least, would sabotage the war effort.

Then on the front page of the *New York Times* for March 24, literally side by side with the story on the conference, was an account of the trial of the eleven communists charged with conspiracy to overthrow the U.S. government by violence. And in that story Fordham Professor Louis F. Budenz (an ex-communist who became a professional anticommunist witness) testified that the American Communist Party did, indeed, demand that its members pay first allegiance to Stalin. It had been the knowledge of Stalin's ruthless purges and imprisonment of their counterparts in Russia that led a faction of intellectuals to oppose the conference, through their own organization, Americans for Intellectual Freedom.

I go into this much detail about this one event, only because it epitomized the rift in the American intellectual

18   Lillian Hellman

left that gave rise to the *Scoundrel Time* controversy and
that still continues. Garry Wills's vitriolic view of the
period in his introduction to *Scoundrel Time*, plus Hellman's own comments on the intellectuals of the anticommunist left, have turned this dinner party of almost
thirty years ago into an historical confrontation. Hellman's chief supporters now are younger than she—they
were children at that time. Her opponents are her contemporaries who were there, many of whom vigorously
survive today to challenge her.[6]

Miss Hellman had heard rumors as early as 1948
that she was on a secret Hollywood blacklist of film em-
ployees—actors, writers, directors, editors—who were not
to be employed in the industry because of suspected
communist affiliation or procommunist sympathies. Then,
in 1949, her name appeared on a list of alleged pro-
communists—"fellow travelers"—investigated by a committee headed by California State Senator Jack Tenney.
Hellman was in famous company: Charles Chaplin, Pearl
Buck, Katherine Hepburn, Danny Kaye, and of course,
Dashiell Hammett, among others, were also on that list.
In 1951, Hammett would be sentenced to six months in
jail for contempt, having refused to name contributors
to the bail-bond fund of the Civil Rights Congress, a
fund set up to supply bail for jailed communists. This
was one of the organizations on the Attorney General's list
of communist fronts. In *An Unfinished Woman* Hellman
says that Hammett had never been in the office of the
Congress and did not know the name of a single contributor, but he went to jail rather than break silence.
And that same year, 1951, an ex-communist screen writer
named Martin Berkeley placed Hellman's name on a list
of one hundred Hollywood "members at large" of the
Communist Party and identified her as one of those attending a meeting of the party at his home in 1937. (In
Scoundrel Time she denies both allegations.) She was not

surprised, then, when she was summoned to appear before the House Un-American Activities Committee in May of 1952.

This congressional committee had begun its activities as far back as 1938 when it was known as the Dies Committee, named for its chairman, Martin Dies, Jr., Democrat of Texas. The committee had blossomed in the 1940s, during World War II and after, in response to popular fears of both fascist and communist subversion of democracy from within, rather than to threats of dictatorship from without. (The armed services and intelligence agencies could take care of that).

After World War II, the concern focused on communist rather than Fascist activity. The House Un-American Activities Committee searched out communist influences on the arts, sciences, and professions, while Senator Joseph McCarthy[7] played upon fears that communists were making or influencing policy within the State Department, the Army, and other official agencies of government.

In 1947, under the chairmanship of J. Parnell Thomas (himself shortly to be convicted of defrauding the government), HUAC had aimed its guns at "Communist infiltration of the Motion Picture Industry." The investigations revealed that indeed some film people had—like many liberals—turned toward communism at one time in their lives. Some had bought the party line and continued to follow it, jockeying for position in the Screen Writer's Guild. Of the nineteen witnesses called before the committee in its most spectacular hearings, the Hollywood Ten were avowed communists who aggressively challenged the constitutionality of HUAC itself and its questioning of witnesses. The courts upheld the right of Congress to work through such a committee, and the Hollywood Ten were found guilty of contempt.

But before the verdict was handed down, fifty executives of the film industry met secretly and drew up a resolution to the effect that the unfriendly ten would be discharged or suspended, and that "unrepenting Communists would no longer be considered suitable for employment in the movies."[8]

The threat of loss of income and professional standing made some leftists quickly "repentant"; others had already become sincerely disillusioned. Among these latter were the idealistic Marxists who were shocked by the ruthless separation of ends from means in the actual workings of the party. As "friendly witnesses" to HUAC, any who confessed, or who testified freely about their own actions, were often obliged to implicate others. For if a witness answered a given question, he could then be required to answer related questions. "Disclosure of a fact waives the privilege as to details." Thus, for example, if the witness admitted to having attended a meeting, he might then be asked to affirm or deny a list of names of others who attended that meeting. If he refused, he could, in the judgment of the Committee, be cited for contempt; and in the event that a court of law upheld the Committee's decision, could be convicted and sentenced. The maximum penalty would be one year in prison and a thousand dollar fine.

Hellman's full account of her appearance before HUAC is the subject of *Scoundrel Time*. Suffice it to say here that in a letter to the Committee she expressed her willingness to discuss her own activities, but not to answer questions about those of anyone else: not to "bring bad trouble to people who in my past association with them, were completely innocent of any talk or any action that was disloyal or subversive." Obviously, however, according to the law, the only way she could avoid answering such questions was to plead the privilege of the Fifth Amendment: to refuse to testify about her own activities on the grounds of self-incrimination. This refusal might make her look guilty in the eyes of the Committee and the public, but such was the chance that she and other "unfriendly" witnesses had to take in order to protect their friends and to avoid a possible conviction.

Although she did have to take the fifth, the letter was an effective statement read into the record. It expressed not only Hellman's own code of honor, but that of others in the same position. She escaped citation for contempt, but not the Hollywood blacklist nor the co-incidental discovery by the IRS that an expensive error had been made on her tax returns. The loss of employment for both her and Hammett, and the enormous tax payments due for both, necessitated selling the farm in Pleasantville, which Hellman had owned and loved since 1939. Not until the 1960s was she permitted to work openly for Hollywood again.

In late 1952 and early 1953 the time was certainly ripe for the revival of *The Children's Hour* as a political play. McCarthy was riding high, and his technique of the blatant lie or rumored suspicion had caused the same devastation in many lives that took place in that play. The new *Children's Hour* was a success, but the proceeds went chiefly to the Internal Revenue Service.

That summer of 1953 Hellman went to Rome to work on a movie for Alexander Korda, at one-fifth of her pre-blacklisting salary. But even that contract fizzled because of the producer's own financial troubles. In the meantime, however, Hellman had experienced passport difficulties, a planted news story that she had been subpoenaed by the McCarthy committee, and being shadowed by an agent of the CIA. (We are told all about this in *Scoundrel Time*). When she returned to the U.S., it was to straitened circumstances—hard times. For a while, she was even forced to take a part-time job in a department store, under a pseudonym. But about six months later she came into an inheritance from one of her New Orleans aunts, and gradually began to write again.

A testimonial to Hellman's tremendous energy is her productivity throughout those stormy years of political activity. After the overnight success of *The Children's Hour*, followed by the depressing failure of *Days to Come* two years later, Hellman turned her hand to screenwriting: she collaborated on *Dark Angel* (United Artists, 1935); wrote a screen version of *The Children's Hour* called *These Three* (United Artists, 1936); and wrote the film script for Sidney Kingsley's *Dead End* (United Artists, 1936). Then in 1939 she completed what is probably her most famous play, *The Little Foxes*. Its success enabled her to buy the farm in Pleasantville, where she and Hammett spent so many productive years. By that time, she had written seven of her eight original plays; had shuttled between New York and Hollywood to work on six films, had made her eventful journeys to Europe, and still had time to play her part in politics and to make Hardscrabble Farm not only a writer's haven for herself, Hammett, and friends, but a going agricultural concern. Life there was to provide important material for the memoirs.

For all her public visibility, Hellman is essentially a private person. In the memoirs we learn what she wants us to know about the significant events and relationships in her life during these years—her psychoanalysis, the death of her parents, her lifelong friendships and contacts. In 1955, she bought a house in Martha's Vineyard and since then has divided her year between that island off the coast of Massachusetts, and New York City.

Hellman's memoirs tell us little about her development as a playwright; for changes in interests and style, we must look to the plays themselves. They fall roughly into two groups: the early melodramas of active villainy, and the later, more discursive plays about characters whose participation in life is essentially passive. Nineteen fifty-one had seen the production of *The Autumn Garden*, a play about middle-aged characters whose lives have simply happened to them—or not happened.

After *The Autumn Garden*, Hellman experimented with adaptations of plays, or plots for plays, by others. She selected congenial material: the originals were all concerned, in one way or another, with an individual's freedom of choice in a milieu alien or hostile to him. But none of the adaptations achieved anything like the success of her own *Toys in the Attic* (1960). For this, her last original play—to date—Hellman returned to the real or imagined past of her own family, or of one remarkably like it. She was moving in the direction of the memoirs.

On her way there, however, (*An Unfinished Woman* was published in 1969) she traveled, wrote magazine articles, collected honors and honorary degrees, and entered academe as a teacher of creative writing and literature. Some of her plays had already won prizes: The Pulitzer went to *The Little Foxes*; the New York Drama Critics Circle Award, to *Watch on the Rhine* and *Toys in the Attic*. Among other honors, between 1960 and 1965, she was elected to the American Academy of Arts and Sciences; the National Institute of Arts and Letters elected her vice-president; and the institute's parent organization, the American Academy of Arts and Letters, invited her to become one of its fifty members. Then the Academy-Institute awarded her its gold medal. Her university awards and honorary degrees included the Brandeis University Creative Arts Award (a medal and $1500), the Achievement Award of the women's division of the Albert Einstein College of Medicine of Yeshiva University, and advanced honorary degrees from Tufts, Wheaton College, Douglass College of Rutgers University, and Brandeis. Later she acquired honorary degrees from (among others) Smith, Holyoke, New York University and Yale.

In 1961, after the triumph of *Toys in the Attic*,

Hellman began teaching at Harvard. That was a sad year for her personally, since Hammett died in January. Professionally, however, this was the beginning of some fifteen years of teaching at prestigious universities including Yale, Massachusetts Institute of Technology, the University of California at Berkeley, and most recently, Hunter College in New York. Her reputation as a teacher, as might be expected, was that of an eclectic scholar and a tough critic of student writing. She was, of course, sympathetic with the rebellious students during the years of unrest and rioting in the late 1960s. In 1968 she was completing work on the first memoir while teaching at Harvard. In 1969 she spoke in defense of the student rioters there—and was later, in the late 1970s, disappointed in the apathy that took the place of the former rebelliousness.

It is not surprising that after the success of *An Unfinished Woman* in 1969, which won the National Book Award in the category of Arts and Letters, Hellman continued to express herself politically. She saw a straight line of descent between the repression of individual rights as she had experienced it at the hands of government through the HUAC, and the attempts of the authorities to stifle the dissent of students and others not only through the police, but through federal agencies such as the FBI and the CIA. The Watergate coverups, to Hellman, only masked a larger conspiracy of secrecy on the part of a government that involved its citizens in a war they did not believe in, and the full extent of which they did not know.

In 1970 Hellman took the lead in founding the Committee for Public Justice. Her idea was "to create an early-warning system that would detect violations of constitutional rights and then alert citizens, the media, and legislators about them."[9] The organization has been doing this and more: has held and published the proceedings of two major conferences[10] and initiated pub-

lication of a newsletter called *Justice Department Watch*.
Many abuses brought to public attention only recently
were revealed long ago by CPJ. Hellman has lent her
influence to raising money for the organization and cur-
rently serves as its cochairman.

Pentimento, the second volume of memoirs, appeared in 1973, and *Scoundrel Time* in 1976. Both were
best sellers, and both have kept Hellman in the public
eye. *Scoundrel Time* not only recounted Hellman's experiences before the HUAC in that time of scoundrels, but
also castigated those of her liberal acquaintances who,
according to Hellman, did not oppose McCarthy or come
to the rescue of his victims. She blamed attitudes of the
anticommunist liberal intellectuals for the sequence of
events from McCarthyism to Vietnam and Watergate. The
original reception of *Scoundrel Time* was as enthusiastic
as that of the other two memoirs. In recent months, however, both the anticommunist left and the conservatives
(as well as some middle-of-the-roaders) have counter-
attacked, and Hellman has become a controversial figure.

The movie, *Julia*, from the episode of that title in
Pentimento, had its New York première with much fanfare. Hellman's instinct for timeliness has made *Julia* one
of the new "woman-flicks" portraying women not as
competing man-traps, but as loyal, loving friends and
political idealists. While Hellman supports the new femi-
nism, she has never felt the need, herself, to be liberated
from the chauvinist male put-down. The real goal of the
movement, she says, should be economic equality. Still,
she is irritated at so frequently being called a "woman
playwright" (even "America's greatest") and has no use
for the "lady writers" of what was once characterized as
women's magazine fiction. Oddly enough, some of her
most devoted followers now are readers of those magazines—educated upper-middle-class matrons who see in
Hellman's career what might have been for them. Other

worshipers are the young feminist writers and artists who consider her an inspiration and a role model.

Hellman has also become a grande dame of the literary establishment in America. She may not be universally liked and admired, but she is known as a presence to be reckoned with. As a playwright she was a major contributor to American theater; now she has become an innovator in the literary form of the memoir.

II
The Plays

1

Hellman's Dramatic Mode—
"The Theater Is a Trick . . ."

Lillian Hellman wrote eight original plays, four adaptations of plays or stories by others, and wrote or collaborated on more than seven screenplays. The original plays fall into two principal groups, based on Hellman's view of human action and motivation—a highly moral view, interpreting both action and the failure to act in terms of good and evil.

The first two plays became signposts, marking the directions to be taken by the later plays. *The Children's Hour* concerned active evil—here the ruin of two women by the spreading of a malicious lie. The drama pointed the way toward the three plays whose chief characters are despoilers—those who exploit or destroy others for their own purposes. Hellman's second play, *Days to Come*, was not so much about the despoilers—the evildoers themselves—as about those characters who, well-meaning or not, stand by and allow the despoilers to accomplish their destructive aims. Often these bystanders may be the victims of their own naiveté or lack of self-knowledge.

The despoiler plays are *The Little Foxes*, *Another Part of the Forest*, and *Watch on the Rhine*. Each is a tightly constructed drama, leading to a violent climax that is the result of evildoing. Most of the characters are clearly defined as evil or good, harmful or harmless. But the so-called bystander plays—*The Searching Wind*, *The Autumn Garden*, and *Toys in the Attic*—are as different

29

from the despoilers in structure as they are in theme. The
action is slower, the plot more discursive and low-keyed,
moving more within the characters and the events that
befall them, than through their actions. For most of
these people are unable to act positively or with conviction. They let things happen and they become the passive victims of the despoilers and themselves. Despoilers
and bystanders appear in some form in all the plays, but
Hellman clearly differentiates between evil as a positive,
rapacious force in the first group, and evil as the negative
failure of good in the second.

Hellman's plays are written in the realistic mode, as
distinguished from "theatricalist." In the history of theater, realism is a fairly recent phenomenon, dating from
the late nineteenth century. The drama of earlier cen-
turies, from the Greeks to the English Restoration, had
been mainly theatrical: that is, it assumed that the theater
was its own small world or microcosm, and that drama
was a unique art form with its own accepted conventions.
The microcosm of the stage reflected the ultimate macrocosm—the universe. The audience expected the actors to
be larger than life (or smaller and cruder, if they were
comic) and to speak with exaggerated tones and gestures.
The actor could address the audience directly in solilo-
quies and asides, or he could drop the part he was playing and speak in his own voice.

By the nineteenth century, theatricalism had produced a theater devoted chiefly to diversion, entertain-
ment, and thrills. The rising demand for verisimilitude in
all the arts seemed urgently necessary in the theater.
Henrik Ibsen in Norway, and August Strindberg in Swe-
den, led the way in the 1870s and 1880s, and were soon
followed by Anton Chekhov and George Bernard Shaw.
The drama of the period became (as it had previously
been with the great theatricalism of the Greeks and
Shakespeare) a serious art form, now concerned with
examining and representing the lives and problems of

real, i.e. contemporary, human beings. Sets became complicated facsimiles of real places, and actors were expected to use the language and gestures typical of real people. Theatricalist form survived, of course, in romantic verse dramas, farces, fantasies, and in the musical theater —from grand opera, to Gilbert and Sullivan, to music-hall vaudeville.

But the new realism did not always produce quality. The assumption that art or the theater should be an imitation of life does not always lead to profundity, nor does the opposite assumption, that art or the theater exists for its own sake, lead necessarily to song-and-dance acts. Realism as a style has been dominant in both good and bad plays and novels from about 1900 to the present. In its early days, it was represented not only by the work of Ibsen and his followers but also in the comedies and melodramas of such playwrights as Dion Boucicault. For the aim of theatrical realism is ultimately to convince the audience, through skillful deception, that they are witnessing real events. The aim of many a nineteenth-century "mellerdrammer" was to make the audiences boo the villains and cheer the heroes as if they were not actors. Popular patterns were often repeated, as they are in that most realistic of modern forms, the television soap opera. Audiences did not need the grandeur of mythical or royal characters when they could identify with brave Mose, the fireman, as he climbed the ladder to save the child crying in the window of the burning house. No *deus ex machina* in *Medea* could match that horse-drawn fire engine clanging and roaring across the stage.

Realism, then, may include any form of drama, from tragedy to drawing-room comedy; it is not a genre but a style or mode. It may also avail itself of symbolic action or language. Movies and television scripts are full of visual puns and symbolic gestures that only enhance the realistic, or photographic, effect. Ordinary speech at its best is full of images and metaphors. But realism on the modern stage makes some assumptions about narrative and about communication not always shared by theatricalism. Realism assumes that there is a certain logical connection between events; that all actions have consequences, if only to disturb the air; that no matter how fragmentary or figurative the dialogue, it has some recognizable meaning to convey. Realism also assumes a clear division between subject and object, on stage and off. A speaker is a subject; a listener on the stage or in the audience is an (indirect) object; all persons are subjects compared to things, which are objects. (Things do not think or talk in realistic drama.) And all people and things are distinct units, separate from one another, and need to be so for us to perceive them clearly.

Theatricalism considers the assumptions of realism to be limitations that theatrical form should try to transcend. And, indeed, no sooner had realism become established than it began to harden into a conventional mold, with its own restricted vision, stereotyped characters, conventional plots, and stock situations. Among the first to realize the limitations of realism was Strindberg, himself, one of the movement's founders. In *The Dream Play* (1902) and *The Ghost Sonata* (1907), Strindberg turned to a form known as expressionism. The action of the play was not modeled on action in a world of concrete reality, but on what takes place in the mind, as projected in dreams or visions. Events followed each other by association, not logic. A stream of events prefigured the stream of consciousness technique in the novel; a stream of scenes—pictures or tableaus—prefigured the technique of projecting a character's thought on the film screen.

Expressionism was only one of many theatrical techniques aimed at overcoming the limitations of realism, but it was a technique that appealed to many of Hellman's immediate precursors and contemporaries. Eugene O'Neill had written expressionistic plays side by side with the realistic ones—both *Anna Christie* (realistic) and *The*

Emperor Jones (expressionistic) were written in 1920. In 1923, Elmer Rice's *The Adding Machine* became the classic example of expressionism in American theater. More recent Americans to experiment with a combination of modes include Arthur Miller, Tennessee Williams, and Edward Albee.

Modern European and American theatricalist forms of drama have gone through innumerable trends and schools, both preceding and following expressionism. Some present a fragmented, nonlogical, nonnarrative view of life, e.g., surrealism, the theater of the absurd, or the sprawling epic. Others annihilate the boundary between audience and stage, demanding audience participation and response as part of the play, i.e., the theater of cruelty, the living theater, and the guerilla theater. Still others use words or situations abstracted from the logic of meaning, words for their own sake, as in Peter Handke's *Sprechstücke*; or situations for their own sake, as in *I*, a "theatrical event only," produced by the Belgian Theatre Laboratoire Vicinal.[1]

Hellman declared for realism at the beginning of her career, and left it only in a couple of adaptations, late in that career. In the introduction to her first published collection (*Four Plays*, 1942) she stated her position. Her argument in that essay is directed at the criticism that she writes "well-made plays"*—plays depending upon the careful structuring of events to create suspense, or as she defines it: "the play whose effects are contrived, whose threads are knit tighter than the threads in life and so do not convince." This charge was leveled at much of her

---

* The term "well-made play" derives originally from the *pièce bien faite*, a form invented by the French playwright Eugene Scribe (1791–1861), and popularized by him in some five hundred plays. They are written to formula, designed by spacing effects to keep the audience expectant throughout. By the late nineteenth centry, the form came to include "clear, neat, balanced, overall construction, and the appearance, at least, of verisimilitude."[2]

work, and her answer was always to the effect that drama as a form demands contrivance, and what does it matter if the play is contrived, as long as it *is* convincing? For the stage, says Hellman, is a

tight, unbending, unfluid, meager form in which to write. . . . [The author] has three walls of a theatre and he has begun his pretense with the always rather comic notion that the audience is the fourth wall. He must pretend and he must represent. And if there is something vaguely awry, for me, about the pretense of representation . . . it is not that I wish to deny to other writers their variations of the form, but that, for me, the realistic form has interested me most.

As to "well-madeness," the theater itself is a trick, according to Hellman, and demands that the playwright "trick up the scene."

This statement, written in 1942, remains definitive. It was not until many years later in the memoirs, and occasionally in interviews, that Hellman spoke again about her playwriting, and about the two men who helped launch her career. Herman Shumlin, for whom she had once read scripts, became the producer of her first five plays. Dashiell Hammett taught her the need for discipline, objectivity, and constant rewriting. This was always to be hard work for Hellman, but she felt that she had an instinct for theater: that the "second-rate form" came naturally to her, while the novel form did not. The memoirs were to be her novel, but they, too, sometimes took the form of plays or screenplays—instinctively theatrical, instinctively well-made.

2

Signposts

THE CHILDREN'S HOUR AND BROADWAY, 1934

American drama was coming of age in the 1930s. The list of famous names among playwrights began, of course, with O'Neill, and included Maxwell Anderson, Robert Sherwood, Phillip Barry, Elmer Rice, Clifford Odets, Paul Green, Marc Connelly, S. N. Behrman, Sidney Howard, Sidney Kingsley, and Thornton Wilder. There were few women: Rachel Crothers and Susan Glaspell had done most of their work in the 1920s or before; Zona Gale was primarily a novelist. Zoë Akins and Rose Franken were Hellman's only female competitors of any stature, and they were what she would call "lady writers."

The realistic mode was far and away the most popular on Broadway in 1934. One hundred and forty-five modern plays were produced in New York City in the season of 1934–1935, not counting plays in the repertories of the Abbey Theater or the Moscow Art Players. Only nine nonmusical plays of the entire season can be called nonrealistic, or theatrical, in mode. But some of the most distinguished writers were experimenting with theatricalism, and the nine plays in that style (mostly pageants or poetry, or fantasy) included work by O'Neill, Sean O'Casey, Paul Green, Marc Connelly, Maxwell Anderson, and Archibald MacLeish. Of the ten best plays of 1934–1935, as selected by Burns Mantle,[1] three were

theatricalist (a high percentage considering the totals
given above) and seven were realistic.

In form, then, Hellman was conventional—but her
material was a different matter. She was just beginning
to formulate her political philosophy and was not yet
ready to make that the theme of a play. But she was ready
to challenge the conventions of a society that destroys
those who deviate from its mores—in this instance,
sexual. And that same conventional society would award
the Pulitzer Prize to a sentimental drama, *The Old Maid*,
by Zoë Akins, instead of to *The Children's Hour*—the
only one of the acceptable candidates to be designated as
"outstanding."

The plot of *The Children's Hour* was based on the
narrative of an actual trial: "Closed Doors; or The Great
Drumsheugh Case," one of a collection of criminal cases
entitled *Bad Companions*, by William Roughead (New
York: Duffield and Green, 1931). The events in the original took place in 1810. Two headmistresses of a genteel
Scottish boarding school for young ladies were accused
of a lesbian attachment to each other, on the lying testimony of a pathologically vindictive sixteen-year-old
schoolgirl. The girl's grandmother believed the accusation and influenced the parents of all the students to
withdraw them from the school. The teachers sued for
libel, and the case dragged on for ten years. Although
they were finally exonerated by the House of Lords, the
teachers were destroyed socially and economically. (Hellman used a few additional details from her source: the
character of the ex-actress aunt of one of the teachers,
a nonexistent keyhole, and the location of the rooms.)

While the theme of *The Children's Hour* was un-
conventional enough to cause a stir among moralists, it
was hardly revolutionary on the stage, historically speaking. Homosexuality had been portrayed in the Renaissance
English drama, and made its appearance on the modern
American stage about 1920. The best-known play on

lesbianism was *The Captive* (1926), a translation from
the French of Edouard Bourdet. *The Captive* achieved
notoriety when it was closed by the New York police; but
it had been preceded by other plays on the subject as
early as 1921. Two of these were concerned with life in
a girls' boarding school—*These Days* (1928) by Katherine Clugston, and an adaptation of Christa Winsloe's
German play, *Girls in Uniform*, produced just the year
before *The Children's Hour*.[2]

Hellman said that *The Children's Hour* was a play
about good and evil. The terms did not apply to the
theme of homosexuality but to that of destructive scandal-
mongering—the smear and the big lie. And, simultane-
ously, to the power of the old and rich to rob—to despoil
—others of livelihood and life.

The machinery leading to the downfall of the two
teachers, Karen Wright and Martha Dobie, is set in motion in Hellman's version by the neurotic child, and completed by the grandmother, as in the Drumsheugh case.
The girl, fourteen-year-old Mary Tilford, hates the school
and all authority, even the reasonable, gentle approach of
the two teachers. She has learned how, by lying and
flattery, to win sympathy from adults, and by bullying to
make tools of her schoolmates.

We are given no reason or motivation for Mary's
hostility. In her manuscript notes[3] for the play, Hellman
compared Mary to Shakespeare's Iago, the villain in
Othello who is traditionally considered to exemplify
"motiveless malignancy." Hellman indicates that Mary is
different from Iago only in her fear of consequences.

Although Mary is the initiating force of evil in the
play, other characters, by their own pride, weakness, and
gullibility, execute her purposes. Most important, of
course, is her wealthy grandmother—rigidly self-righteous
and status-conscious. But there is also Martha's Aunt Lilly
Mortar, a vain ex-actress, dependent upon Martha and
envious of her success. For their own reasons, both these

women are receptive to Mary's lies. Mary's schoolmates
are terrified of her. The terror of one child, Rosalie (who,
Mary knows, has stolen another girl's bracelet), accounts
for Mary's success, through blackmail and intimidation.

Mrs. Mortar is a nuisance at the school, undermining
discipline and irritating the teachers. For respite from
her, they offer Mrs. Mortar a trip to England. In her
anger at this plan, the aunt accuses her niece of opposing
Karen's impending marriage to Dr. Joseph Cardin. This
is a sore point for Martha, because there is some truth
in it: she is afraid of loneliness—in spite of Karen's re-
assurance that the three of them will be together and that
Martha and she will continue to run the school. The
aunt's accusation is explicit:

MRS. MORTAR: I know what I know. Every time that man
    comes into this house, you have a fit. It seems like you
    just can't stand the idea of them being together. God
    knows what you'll do when they get married. You're
    jealous of him, that's what it is.

MARTHA: I'm very fond of Joe, and you know it.

MRS. MORTAR: You're fonder of Karen, and I know that.
    And it's unnatural, just as unnatural as it can be. You
    don't like their being together. You were always like
    that even as a child. If you had a little girl friend, you
    always got mad when she liked anybody else. Well, you'd
    better get a beau of your own now—a woman of your
    age.

Two of the schoolgirls overhear this conversation,
and Mary Tilford bullies them into telling her what was
said. Armed with this information, and the memory of
some passages she has read from *Mademoiselle de Maupin*
(Gautier's titillating novel describing some varieties of
sexual experience—including inversion) Mary runs away
to her grandmother's.

She tries to convince Mrs. Tilford that she is being
persecuted at the school, but her lies are so transparent

that the grandmother sees through them. Even after Mary's
wheedling flattery, "I love you, grandma," etc., the old
lady still insists that the child return to school. Then,
when nothing else works, Mary plays her ace: she tells
Mrs. Tilford about the overheard quarrel between Martha
and Mrs. Mortar, with emphasis on the word "unnatural."
Mary elaborates on the situation from her imagination
and the episodes from *Mademoiselle de Maupin*, suggesting sexual goings-on between Karen and Martha in
Karen's room. Mrs. Tilford panics, and telephones the
parents of other girls, who promptly take their daughters
out of school.

The two teachers and Joe, Karen's fiancé, confront
the grandmother and Mary, and almost succeed in break-
ing down the child's story: she said that she had seen
"things" through a keyhole in Karen's door, and heard
things through the wall in Martha's room. But, as in the
Drumsheugh case, there is no keyhole in that door, and
Martha's room (which she shares with her aunt) is on a
different level, at a far end of the building. But as the
grandmother begins to waver, Mary claims that she got
the story from Rosalie, and Rosalie, afraid that her
"borrowing" of another girl's bracelet will be revealed,
confesses falsely that she had seen and reported the
damaging evidence to Mary.

The teachers bring a libel suit against Mrs. Tilford,
but lose because of the absence of Mrs. Mortar, who refuses to return from her trip to testify. (An absent "bystander," she is afraid of being involved in a scandal.)
The teachers become social outcasts, unable even to leave
the house. The school is ruined, and distrust has even
tainted Karen's engagement to Joe—his protestations to
the contrary. Joe departs, at Karen's insistence that their
marriage would never work and that his suspicions would
never be laid to rest. When Martha hears this, she suddenly admits to Karen—and herself—that she, Martha,
has indeed loved Karen "that way," and that in fact,

the aunt's accusation was true; but Martha herself was not conscious of her feelings until all the trouble.

> "It's funny, it's all mixed up. There's something in you, and you don't know it and you don't do anything about it. Suddenly a child gets bored and lies—and there you are, seeing it for the first time. . . . It all seems to come back to *me*. In some way I've ruined your life. I've ruined my own. I didn't even *know*. . . ."

Karen is shaken by the confession, weeps, and unconsciously—in the Shakespearian manner—suggests Martha's fate: "Go and lie down, Martha. You'll feel better." Martha goes, and a few minutes later a shot is heard; she has committed suicide. Shortly afterward, when Karen and the aunt have discovered Martha's body, Mrs. Tilford arrives. She is old and broken; the black maid, Agatha, persuades Karen to see her. The bracelet has been found in Rosalie's room, and the truth about Mary's blackmail is out. Mrs. Tilford wants to make whatever amends she can, mostly financial. Karen is not interested, but there is a small note of hope at the end of the play—she and Joe Cardin may get back together after all.

Two major objections were raised to the play by well-known critics—among others, Brooks Atkinson of the *New York Times*, reviewing the 1934 production, and Eric Bentley, reviewing the 1952 version. The two agreed, essentially, that the play should have ended with the pistol shot, or even before. Atkinson said, "When two people are defeated by the malignance of an aroused public opinion, leave them the dignity of their hatred and despair."[4] In her introduction to *Four Plays*, Miss Hellman acknowledged that perhaps the play should have ended with the suicide, but added: "I am a moral writer, often too moral a writer, and I cannot avoid, it seems, that last summing-up."

The second objection is related to this answer. Bentley was unhappy that Hellman supposedly established the premise that the two women were "innocent," and then shifted ground by making one of them "guilty."[5]

But Hellman carefully prepared her audience in act one for Martha's final revelation. Martha is portrayed as depressed and fearful at the prospect of Karen's marriage. Moreover, in Hellman's source, *Bad Companions*, the author-editor, William Roughead, had declared emphatically (his italics), "My interest in the case resides in the fact that *the charge was false*." Roughead was apologizing for handling such a distasteful subject at all, but this is just the kind of statement that would inspire Hellman to react with the opposite view. What if the charge were *not* false? What if, after all, one—or even both—women had such feelings, consciously or unconsciously? Would the "guilty" deserve destruction at the hands of society? Changing mores between 1934 and 1978, and the open treatment of homosexuality on the stage and elsewhere today, make the answer for most audiences, clearly, no. In fact, it is ironic that this most outspoken and revolutionary play in its time should now seem so old-fashioned.

The play may have lost the Pulitzer Prize because of its theme, and been banned in Boston and, for a while, in Chicago and London, but New York audiences supported it for 691 performances—an astounding record for a first play. After eighty-six weeks in New York, the play went on tour here and abroad for another year.

The Children's Hour was twice made into a motion picture. The first, 1936, was called *These Three*, and Miss Hellman herself rewrote it as a love triangle, omitting, as censorship demanded, the homosexual theme. In 1962 another version was filmed, using the original title and restoring the lesbian relationship. One can still see *These Three* on the late show on television, but the movie called *The Children's Hour* seems to have disappeared. And

probably for good reason, since most of the critics found
it clumsy and embarrassing; Hellman herself preferred
the censored movie version.

In the 1952 revival Hellman directed the play herself,
to point up the analogy between the destructive forces in
The Children's Hour and those represented by McCarthy
and the House Un-American Activities Committee. The
smear technique and the big lie now became applicable
to the witch hunt for communists, but again, the double
question was raised: What if the accused *were* communists? How bad was that? In *Scoundrel Time*, Hellman
was to say that she thought it was not nearly as bad as
being a member of the anticommunist liberal left: intellectuals who, Hellman said, gave indirect support to
McCarthy and all he represented. This argument, as we
shall see, has brought down a tempest on her head: the
gays and the straights may be reconciled in 1978, but
not the factions of the old and new political left—much
less those of the left and right.

Characterization in all Hellman's plays is trenchant,
and her characters are looked at, objectively, from the
outside; the playwright sees them but does not identify
with them. Unlike many playwrights—O'Neill is the most
obvious example—she does not use the stage to express
her innermost, personal conflicts or sufferings; she is
singularly intolerant of self-pity wherever she sees it.
With a few exceptions, her compassion and empathy were
to be saved for the memoirs, and there, too, it is highly
selective. Even the persona of herself—the "I" who remembers and the "Lillian" who acts—is sometimes mocked
in the memoirs and the plays. In a recent interview, Hellman commented on this critical attitude toward herself.
She was discussing her difficulties with psychoanalysis:
"The man who analyzed me once said I was the only
patient he'd ever had in his life who talked about herself
as if I [sic] were another person. He meant no compliment. He meant that I had too cold a view of myself."[6]

In the introduction to *Four Plays*, Hellman says that she saw some of Mary, the *enfant terrible*, in herself and her early experience: "I reached back into my own childhood and found the day *I* finished *Mlle. de Maupin*; the day *I* faked a heart attack; the day *I* saw an arm get twisted." (In fact, in *Pentimento*, Lillian herself does a bit of arm-twisting on another girl, one Christy Houghton.) "And I thought again," she added, "of the world of the half-remembered, the half-observed, the half-understood which you need so much as you begin to write."

Hellman's portraits of the two women in *The Children's Hour*, especially of Martha, seem to have been drawn also from this half-remembered world. The rebelliousness of the young Lillian in the memoirs is often rooted in jealousy—sometimes in an adolescent crush on an adult of either sex, or a close relationship to another girl, the "beloved friend," Julia, of *Pentimento*. Hellman was to be as honest and outspoken about that in the memoirs as she was about her irritability and brattishness. By 1934, whatever was sexual in the Lillian-Julia relationship had been outgrown, or suppressed or sublimated; Hellman was living with Hammett, and Julia was studying medicine in Vienna (where Dr. Joe Cardin of *The Children's Hour* also studied.) But when Julia was maimed in an explosion, and Lillian sat at her bedside, Hellman's complicated, half-understood feelings must have given her some insight into Martha Dobie—one of the few Hellman characters whose fate could be called tragic. For if the villainy of Mary was, to Hellman, like that of Iago, then the suicide of Martha, in her self-hatred for what she could not help, was like that of Othello, who could not live with what he had seen in himself. *The Children's Hour* and, possibly, *Watch on the Rhine* are the only plays that approach the definition of tragedy, in the Aristotelian sense. Miss Hellman's customary detachment from her characters is related to the genre in which she writes—not tragedy, but "serious drama" or melodrama. For tragedy requires a protagonist whose fall—partly through his own fault, partly through circumstances beyond his control—can excite pity or terror in the spectator. Detachment, objectivity, or simple dislike or hatred rule out such emotional involvement.

Hellman never claimed to be writing classic tragedy, but she *was* writing more than is usually meant by melodrama. Her serious plays are always about good and evil, and evil may seem to prosper unjustly, but the actions and the strivings of the characters have meaning and consequence. Violence is there for a purpose, not just for sensational effect. In the introduction to *Four Plays*, Hellman makes this distinction:

I think the word melodrama, in our time, has come to be used in an almost illiterate manner. By definition it is a violent dramatic piece, with a happy ending. But I think we can add that it uses its violence for no purpose, to point no moral, to say nothing in say-nothing's worst sense. . . . But when violence is actually the needed stuff of the work and comes toward a large enough end, it has been and always will be in the good writer's field. . . . There is a needed return to the correct use of the word melodrama. It is only then the critic will be able to find out whether a writer justifies his use of violence, and to scale him against those who have used it.

Melodrama, as Hellman used the term, was a logical outcome of realism in drama. For in tragedy, some mysterious, often supernatural force, hovers over the action, partly, at least, controlling human destiny. In the mode called naturalism the forces of destruction are also beyond human control, but they are not mysterious. Naturalism depicts life as predetermined by social, economic, or biological forces. Realism, however, assumes that life is seldom mysterious, seldom predetermined. When, in most of Hellman's plays, human beings fail or are destroyed, the powers of destruction are in human hands; they are not functions of a higher necessity or fate, or of naturalistic forces. One reason that *The Children's Hour* is closer to tragedy than most of Hellman's plays is that the evil motivation of Mary, and the psychological drives of Martha, are both outside immediate logical human understanding or control. But it is clear enough that these forces are allowed to triumph by human machination and human weakness. Mary is the first of the despoilers—the foxes who "spoil our vines"—and her accomplices in evil are the self-righteousness in Mrs. Tilford and cowardice in Mrs. Mortar.

In summary, then, *The Children's Hour* has many of the qualities of Hellman's later plays. Its mode and setting are realistic; its characters, strongly etched; its theme, serious; and its tone, indignant. The object of that indignation was both social and individual—a society made up of a group of individuals so bound by their own mores and conventions as to feel compelled, for the preservation of that society, to punish those who deviated from it. But this "society" is general and diffused, not limited to any one class: the blue-collar Archie Bunkers are just as intolerant of deviation from the sexual norm as are the uppercrust Mrs. Tilfords.

It is not until the curtain falls on *The Children's Hour* that one realizes the irony of the opening lines, quoted from *The Merchant of Venice*: "It is twice blest; it blesseth him that gives and him that takes. . . ." The reference, of course, is to mercy, singularly lacking in those who implement the destruction of others. Mercy has nothing to do with political persuasion or social strata: "it droppeth as the gentle rain from heaven" and is "an attribute of God himself." The principle is ethical, moral, Christian—not political. But for many playwrights in the 1930s, human suffering and exploitation was political in origin, and political reform alone could do battle with it. In her next play, *Days to Come*, Hellman made a brief foray into the melee of class struggle.

DAYS TO COME

No intellectual could live through the decade from 1929
to 1939, beginning with the great depression and ending
with World War II, without a concern for social action—
for the plight of the poor, the victims of the capitalistic
system, and of the oppressed, the victims of political
tyranny. Many playwrights felt that serious writing must
treat these problems. The proletarian and activist theater
became a movement, operating through both amateur and
professional groups. The amateurs might be offshoots of
the unions or other labor causes, chanting their messages
at strikes or rallies. Professional playwrights, actors, and
production staff formed groups not only for propaganda
purposes, but to set standards of high quality, to give
each other encouragement, and to provide their members
some measure of economic security. The most well-known
and effective of these (and there were many) were probably The Group Theater, The Union Theater, The Theater
Guild, and the Playwrights' Company. The Federal Theater Project, established in 1935 to provide jobs for
actors, playwrights and technicians, produced many activist plays.

Hellman might have joined any of these groups, but
did not. She stayed with the independent Broadway
theater even in the production of *Days to Come* (1936),
a play on the theme of labor unionization. Thirty-one
plays (twenty-one percent of the total) on Broadway
that season—1935–1936—were on social or political
themes.[7] The most famous of the leftist, pro-labor battle
cries was Clifford Odets's immensely popular *Waiting
for Lefty* (1935).

In her later work, Hellman was to be drawn to causes
only indirectly related to labor or the proletariat: the
ruthless decadence of the southern capitalist in *The Little
Foxes* and *Another Part of the Forest*, and the atrocities

of fascism in *Watch on the Rhine* and *The Searching Wind*. Most of the social action plays on the Broadway stage in the 1930s had a generally liberal or populist orientation. They were not only realistic in form but theatricalist also, from the lighthearted labor-union musical, *Pins and Needles*, to heavy verse tragedy (Maxwell Anderson's *Winterset*), historical drama (Robert Sherwood's *Abe Lincoln in Illinois*), or fantasy (Paul Green's *Johnny Johnson*). *Days to Come*, however, took Hellman's characteristic form—realistic melodrama. The play was a failure, partly because as Hellman said, she tried to say too much about the people in it. The labor cause was not enough to unify the action; Hellman had to explore the individual characters who were themselves often confused about their own motives. There were plot confusions, too —"accidental judgments, casual slaughters . . . purposes mistook" that did not necessarily, as in *Hamlet*, fall on "the inventors' heads," but on everybody's.

The play is set in a small town in Ohio, in which workers are reluctantly striking against their paternalistic employer, Andrew Rodman, part owner of a brush factory, a family business inherited from his father. Hard times have forced Rodman to cut the workers' wages below the poverty level. Some of the less paternalistic stockholders—Henry Ellicott, the family's lawyer, and Rodman's sister, Cora—have persuaded Rodman to break the strike by importing professional strikebreakers, who are mobsters and jailbirds.

The union organizer, Leo Whalen, warns his men not to allow themselves to be provoked by the strikebreakers into rioting or other violence. A long stand-off results, and the gang leader plants the dead body of one of his men, killed in a gambling quarrel, at Union Headquarters. The workers and Whalen are made to look guilty of the murder, and a pretext is established for the strikebreakers to attack the workers. In the ensuing violence, the child of the foreman, Firth, an old friend of

the Rodman family, is killed. The town is torn apart with
shooting, the workers are hungry and tired, and they
agree to call off the strike. They go back to work and
Whalen gives up the attempt to organize a union.

The plot of the play as a whole is as abortive as
Whalen's efforts. It is crowded with loosely related
elements, including blackmail, adultery, and broadly
satirical sketches of the rich. Rodman, the benevolent
manufacturer and reluctant oppressor, turns out to be a
well-meaning but unbelievably naive cuckold. His wife's
ex-lover is Henry Ellicott, the foxiest of little foxes, and
the wife now has a yen for Whalen. Cora, Rodman's sister
and co-owner of the factory, is portrayed as a frustrated
spinster, and as a caricature of the snobbish, greedy, idle
rich. Hellman said in the introduction to *Four Plays* that
she had known prototypes of these characters—had hated
the sister, Cora, pitied the wife, Julie, and respected Leo
Whalen. She "had been raised with the Ellicotts of this
world," presumably the Newhouses, whom we will meet
again in *The Little Foxes.*

All these characters, good and bad, are ineffectual;
and their efforts, along with the plot, just peter out. The
hired thugs accomplish the villainous purpose for which
they are—finally—paid, and leave town. The strike fails,
the unionization fails, the company will probably go
broke, and the marriage of the well-meaning Rodman is
bankrupt. His wife's adulterous affair with Ellicott has
gone sour, and her mawkish attraction to Whalen comes
to nothing. The workers have gone back to their tedious,
underpaid jobs, and the Rodmans go back to their tedious,
trapped, unsatisfying lives. The application of the title
Days to Come to the play is vague. It may have been
intended, like much of the book of Ecclesiastes from
which it was quoted, as a comment on labor and reward.[8]
However, it is a sharper comment on the fate of the characters in the play: "For there is no remembrance of the
wise more than of the fool forever; seeing that which is

in the days to come shall all be forgotten. And how dieth the wise man? As the fool." (Ecclesiastes 2:16)

Days to Come lasted only seven performances, but it was a harbinger of Hellman plays to come. The war between forces of good and evil, with evil the victor, in *The Children's Hour*, had made for a tightly constructed series of conflicts, crises, and resolutions. But Hellman said that *Days to Come* was about evil "in the hands of those who don't understand it," and in Hellman's scheme, ignorance is no excuse—sad, regrettable, but weak, and ultimately destructive. A play based on this proposition must be comparatively discursive and undramatic. The forces of good have no direction except muddle and neglect, and the only reward of such failure is a dim self-insight, when it is too late to reform. "And how dieth the wise man? As the fool."

As Hellman grew older, the more her misanthropy became like that of the preacher in Ecclesiastes, cynical and sad, rather than angry and rebellious. The anger that she had turned against the Tilfords of this world—Mary and her grandmother in *The Children's Hour*—rages through *The Little Foxes* and *Watch on the Rhine*, and flares up again, but almost as parody, in *Another Part of the Forest*. But in *The Searching Wind*, *The Autumn Garden*, and *Toys in the Attic*, Hellman is looking at the Rodmans of the world: the ineffectual ones who let evil and decay attack and destroy the lives of others, as it consumes their own vitality.

3

○○○○○○○○○○○○○○○ ○○○○○○○○○○○○○○○○○○○○○○ ○○○○○○○○○○○○○○

Despoilers

THE LITTLE FOXES

Badly shaken by the failure of *Days to Come*, Hellman took great care with the preparation of *The Little Foxes*. She filled two notebooks with research materials on southern economics, history, and culture; then struggled through nine drafts of the play itself.[1] But it was not just fear of another failure that made her so cautious; it was the personal nature of her source—her own family background. In *Pentimento* Hellman said,

Some of the trouble came because the play has a distant connection to my mother's family and everything. . . . had formed a giant tangled time-jungle in which I could find no space to walk without tripping over old roots, hearing old voices speak about histories made long before my day.

Among the voices were those of Hellman's mother, who appears as the gentle, helpless Birdie (and as Lavinia in *Another Part of the Forest*), and of her grandmother, Sophie Newhouse, and Sophie's aggressive brother, Jake. They are imagined here as Regina and Ben, and would appear in later plays in the characters of hardheaded, shrewd, witty women, and empire-building men. Hellman meant the young girl, Alexandra, to be a "half-mockery" of herself at that age. More specific identification of the Newhouses in this and later plays must wait for later biographies. (Hellman said recently that some of her family had threatened to sue for libel after the play appeared.)

The title, suggested by Dorothy Parker, comes from the Song of Solomon 2:15. "Take us the foxes, the little foxes, that spoil the vines, for our vines have tender grapes." The "foxes" who despoil the land of the south are the Hubbard family. Hellman makes the point that they are the aggressive ones, but there had been, and would be, many others after them just as bad as they were—those who would stand by and watch them "eat the earth."

The Hubbards are Regina and her two brothers, Ben and Oscar. Their father left all his money to the two sons. Regina has married Horace Giddens, a banker, to recoup her financial losses. The Giddens have a daughter, Alexandra, sixteen. All the Hubbards have one passion— money. It is the basis of Oscar's marriage as well as of Regina's. He married the sweet but helpless Birdie, to acquire her aristocratic family's plantation for the Hubbards. He and Birdie have an amoral son, Leo, who works in Horace's bank, whom Oscar hopes to marry off to Alexandra.

The elder and more powerful of the Hubbard brothers is the bachelor, Ben; but if he is king of the clan, Regina is queen, and Horace is her consort.

The action takes place in a town in the deep south in 1900. Hellman had done her homework, as the notebooks testify, on the rise of southern industry, which was beginning at that time to compete with the industry of New England. The industrial revolution is the backdrop against which the "foxes" play their human—or inhuman —roles, much as the rise of labor unionism formed the backdrop for *Days to Come*. As in that play, audience interest is much less in what the characters have done to society than in what they have done to each other.

Hellman moves them like chessmen: first one, then the other seizes power. And since power is a function of money, to understand the moves, one has to understand the dollar figures. The family has made a deal with a Chicago industrialist, Marshall, to set up a cotton mill in the town. Marshall has put up forty-nine percent of the money, and the three Hubbards will put up the remaining fifty-one percent. Regina's, of course, will come from her banker husband, Horace. But Horace, who is being treated for a heart ailment in the hospital at Johns Hopkins, has not come up with his share of the money. The brothers threaten to cut Regina out and find another partner if the money is not forthcoming, but Regina knows that they do not want to take in a stranger. She lets them think that Horace is holding out for a larger controlling share—even though he will pay only one-third of the total—and that she will not persuade him to give the money at all unless he has twice the share promised. Ben gets her to accept forty percent, the extra seven percent of control coming from Oscar's share. To palliate Oscar, the other two agree to encourage his son, Leo, to marry Zan (Alexandra) and thus keep the extra profits at least in the family.

Regina sends Alexandra to the hospital in Baltimore to bring her father home, knowing that he will not refuse his daughter, even though he is too ill to travel. But when they arrive, Horace still refuses to contribute to the scheme, more stubbornly than ever when he learns that part of the deal is a guarantee to Marshall of cheap power and labor, obtainable only, in Horace's words, "by pounding the bones of this town."

With Leo's help, the brothers steal bonds worth $88,000 from Horace's safe-deposit box, bonds which are as negotiable as money, and Oscar takes them to Chicago to make up the missing third of the investment. They let Regina think an outsider has come up with the money. She bullies and threatens Horace, who says she will get no money for this investment from him as long as he lives. Her answer is, "I hope you die. I hope you die soon. . . . I'll be waiting for you to die."

Horace discovers the theft of the bonds, and makes sure that Leo knows. Then he tells Regina of the theft. He adds that he will not report it to the authorities, but will tell the brothers that the bonds are a loan from Regina. When he changes his will, as he plans to do, the bonds will be all she inherits. Regina is trapped; she will receive nothing from her brothers except as they choose to pay back the "loan." But the next move is hers. In the course of their quarrel she and Horace go over their past. She tells him that she has always had only contempt for him. Horace has a heart attack, reaches for his medicine, but spills it. He asks Regina to call the maid, Addie, to get the other bottle, upstairs. But Regina just looks at him. He calls Addie in panic, then tries to climb the stairs, and collapses. When she is sure that he is unconscious, she calls the servants.

The brothers arrive. Leo tells them that Horace knows about the theft. Regina tells them that she knows about it also. Now she has the upper hand: "I'm smiling, Ben. I'm smiling because you are quite safe while Horace lives. But I don't think Horace will live. And if he doesn't live I shall want seventy-five percent in exchange for the bonds. . . . And if I don't get what I want I am going to put all three of you in jail."

But Alexandra comes in to announce that Horace has died and asks her mother, "What was Papa doing on the staircase?" The implications of her question are not lost on Ben, who threatens to use them eventually against his sister. But Regina is still the queen; the princess, Alexandra, refuses to stay with her, to watch the foxes "eat the earth." The only suggestion of vulnerability in Regina now is her invitation to Alexandra to sleep in the same room with her. To which her daughter replies, "Are you afraid, Mama?" The curtain falls.

The plot of *The Little Foxes* consists of a series of crises, each one only partly resolved, so that the audience is kept waiting for the resolution to be completed, only to be surprised or shocked by a reversal, leading to a new crisis. The climax is reached in the quarrel and the death of Horace. Then comes the dénouement—the unraveling in which a few raveled strands remain. This is how well-made melodrama works. Nothing is inevitable, everything is a surprise, and every step in the plot is willed and carried out by human beings. Hellman herself made this point in a newspaper commentary a few days after the opening of *The Little Foxes*:

If you believe, as the Greeks did, that man is at the mercy of the gods he might offend and who will punish him for the offense, then you write tragedy. The end is inevitable from the beginning. But if you believe that man can solve his problems and is at nobody's mercy, then you will probably write melodrama.[2]

But even as relentless a moralist as Hellman had to admit that "man" consists of both victors and victims. In *The Little Foxes*, the fate of the weaker characters shows up the viciousness of the strong in sharp relief. Horace is not entirely a victim; he too was once a despoiler but he is now relenting of his past at the point of death. But Oscar's wife, Birdie, *is* the pathetic victim. She may be weak-willed, but she is also sensitive and musical, with longings for beauty and affection. Horace and Alexandra understand Birdie; they have some of the same longings. (Horace even cherishes a piece of his old violin in his safe-deposit box, with the bonds!)

Audiences suffered with Birdie when they saw her treatment at the hands of Oscar, and pitied her even when she confessed that she drank in private. (That confession scene has always been a cherished one for actresses.) And audiences sympathized with Alexandra, and cheered her when she broke away from the clan, refusing to stay with Regina. But Hellman, as always, had meant to be tough on weak and strong alike, and was surprised by audience reactions. In *Pentimento*, she described her intentions: "I had meant to half-mock my own youthful high-class innocence in Alexandra. . . ." Elsewhere she said, "To my great surprise, the ending of the play was taken to be a statement of faith in Alexandra. . . . I never meant it that way. She did have courage enough to leave, but she would never have the force or vigor of her mother's family."[3]

As to Birdie, "I had meant people to smile at, and to sympathize with, the sad, weak Birdie, certainly I had not meant them to cry." And as for the foxes themselves, "I had meant the audience to recognize some part of themselves in the money-dominated Hubbards; I had not meant people to think of them as villains to whom they had no connection."[4]

It is to Hellman's credit as a writer of realistic drama that audiences listened to her characters more attentively than they did to implied sermons and generalizations. They felt the power of evil in the play and the excitement of each twist of the plot. But in 1939 most critics, as opposed to the audiences, heard the play's message about social conditions in the South. George Jean Nathan's review was fairly typical. He praised Hellman as the foremost among American women playwrights:

She has a dramatic mind, an eye for character, a fundamental strength and a complete and unremitting integrity that are rare among native playwrights of her sex. . . . From first to last, "The Little Foxes" betrays not an inch of compromise, not a sliver of a sop to the comfortable acquiescence of Broadway or Piccadilly, not the slightest token that its author had anything in her purpose but writing the truest and most honest play on her theme that it was possible for her to write.[5]

In 1941, the play was made into a movie, with Bette Davis in the role of Regina, and can still be seen occasionally on television. In 1949 it became an opera, *Regina*, composed by Marc Blitzstein. Since then, *The Little Foxes* has become a standard item of American repertory, amateur and professional. Its first and most impressive professional revival took place in 1967 at Lincoln Center. Audiences were enthusiastic, and the limited engagement at the Center was so oversubscribed that the play had to be moved to a Broadway theater for an additional forty performances, before it began a successful road tour.

But the opinions of the critics in 1967 were divided, and none were neutral; they went from panegyric to panning. Even two *New York Times* critics, Clive Barnes and Walter Kerr, took opposite views of the play, although both were ecstatic over the production. Barnes thought the play was still "well-turned, machine-made" melodrama. But Kerr hailed it as valid Americana, a classic performed with such genius as to provide hope for an American National Theater, a native repertory theater that would be based at Lincoln Center. Miss Hellman repaid Barnes and Kerr, in kind, in *Pentimento* when she said, "Barnes is a 'fashion-swinger'. . . . but. . . . he can't quite find where the swing is located for the new season. Kerr is the only critic on the *Times* who learned and thrived."

The performances of the actors excited as much intense comment, pro and con, as did the play—partly because Mike Nichols, the director, had reinterpreted or updated some of the parts. As for the play as literature, it no longer seemed to carry the populist implications that it had in the 1930s, nor to be a historical record: it was just a play about the evil men do to each other. A minor controversy arose when Elizabeth Hardwick attacked *Foxes*, and Hellman's work generally, in a rather turgid essay in the *New York Review of Books*.[6] The play was poor southern history, the characters were not well-motivated, and the production was not all that interesting or important. Hardwick was immediately answered in the

Review by other critics, friends of Hellman, who came
to her defense—Edmund Wilson, Richard Poirier, and
Penelope Gilliat. Wilson's reply took the form of "An
Open Letter to Mike Nichols"[7] in which he sang the same
hymn of praise as did Walter Kerr, also hoping the production might lead the way to an American National
Theater, in which *The Little Foxes* would be a classic.

And a classic it became.

ANOTHER PART OF THE FOREST

Hellman had originally intended to write a trilogy of
plays about the Hubbards. *The Little Foxes* would be in
the middle: *Another Part of the Forest* was to cover the
Hubbards' past, and a third play was to take them up
through the 1930s. But Hellman said she was tired of the
Hubbards after *Another Part of the Forest*, so she never
wrote the third play. Although seven years and two
other plays intervened, the Hubbard plays are best described in relation to each other.

In *Another Part of the Forest*, Hellman takes the
family history back only one generation to 1880. The
father and mother, Marcus and Lavinia, are still alive.
Marcus scorns and ridicules his wife, and will be Oscar's
model for his treatment of Birdie in *The Little Foxes*. At
this point, however, none of the children is married; the
two boys have menial low-paying jobs in the Hubbard
business, and Marcus intends to keep it that way. He
lavishes his money on Regina, who spends it on expensive clothes from Chicago. The family is known to the
townspeople as ruthless, bigoted, and penny-pinching,
having made its money during the civil war at the expense
of its own neighbors. In contrast to the Hubbards are
the Bagtrys—Birdie, her mother, and her cousin, John
Bagtry. They are land and cotton poor, starving on their
plantation, Lionnet, and because of their aristocratic
heritage and manners, a thorn in the side of the Hubbards.

Hellman's aim, she said, was not to write history, but to try to understand what lay behind the behavior of the Hubbards, "to look into their family background and to find out what it was that made them the nasty people they were." She had, then, to use a psychological approach. Hellman, herself, was in analysis at the time and dedicated the play to Gregory Zilboorg, her psychoanalyst.

The nastiness of the Hubbards begins in the play with Marcus, a brutal "primal father" of his tribe, such as Freud described in *Totem and Taboo*. The drama becomes a contest between the father and the oldest son, Ben, who crushes the father in the end and takes his place. The sibling rivalry between Ben and Oscar turns into a kind of one-sided Cain and Abel struggle, in which the older brother subdues the younger and weaker. (Oscar is not only amoral, he is also stupid.) In her father's affections, Regina has displaced her mother, Lavinia, who considers herself—as her husband does—violated and soiled by her marriage to him. The father's attachment to his daughter is given incestuous overtones, and there is more than a hint that Ben is a jealous rival of his father for Regina, as well as for his money. (Maybe this is why Ben remains a bachelor, and, in *The Little Foxes*, lives next door to his sister and the weak husband he chose for her.)

The financial tricks the Hubbards play on each other need not concern us here. Suffice it to say that they attempt to enslave and exploit each other just as they have done, and will do, to the townspeople and the Bagtrys. The only passion for any of them, outside of money, is lust, and they easily make their peace with sex when cash is the substitute. Oscar is in love—"deeply and sincerely" he keeps saying—with the town prostitute. One of the comic, or satiric, highlights of the play occurs when Oscar brings his girlfriend to meet the family. But Ben soon breaks up that affair and sets the scene for

Oscar to court Birdie Bagtry, and bring those rich cotton fields into the family. Oscar's broken heart is soon on the mend at the prospect of being rich.

Regina is in love, too, at the beginning of the play. She has been having an affair with the penniless John Bagtry, and hopes to get him to elope with her to Chicago, since she knows that neither her father nor Ben would ever approve a marriage. (John is, after all, only a cousin of the Bagtrys and would not inherit the plantation.) But John is essentially a man of honor, an officer and a gentleman, who was happy only during the war when he was in the army.* John's affair with Regina is beginning to pale, and all he wants now is to go to Brazil to fight in a war brewing there. When John is, finally, out of the picture, Regina aligns herself with the money and power; first with her father, and at the end, with Ben.

The climax of the play and the defeat of Marcus is brought about by Lavinia, his downtrodden wife. The audience has the pleasure—rare in a Hellman play—of watching virtue triumph or at least, find its own reward. Lavinia is a bit dotty, in a religious way, but she is a woman of courage and principle, under all her submissiveness. She has always been afraid of her husband and Ben, too:

> "I spent a life afraid. And you know that's funny, Benjamin, because way down deep I'm a woman wasn't made to be afraid. . . . I'm not afraid to die. . . . and if you're not afraid of dying then you're not afraid of anything."

For years she has been begging Marcus to build her a little schoolhouse in Altaloosa, where she can fulfill her mission in life, to teach black children. (And not the Bible, either. They are too young to read about what goes

---

* Hellman said that Dashiell Hammett was the first man she had ever known who flourished in military service. Such honorable soldiers, or would-be soldiers, appear in several of her plays.

on in that book!) Lavinia's only friendship and support have come from the blacks and their churches, and she and Coralee, her maid, share the secret that destroys Marcus. When he has refused, year after year, to listen to her plea, and has threatened to send her away to a mental hospital, Lavinia makes up her mind to escape. Ben is leaving, and she demands that he take her with him as far as Altaloosa.

Ben is reluctant until his mother gradually gives him the information about his father's past that could hang Marcus if it became known in the town. The townspeople already hate him for exploiting them during the civil war; selling badly needed salt, smuggled through the blockade, for extortionary black-market prices. Moreover, the townspeople have suspected that he led the Union troops to a camp where southern boys—sons and brothers of the local folks—were training, and where the Yankees slaughtered twenty-seven boys, including John Bagtry's twin. Marcus has always had an alibi to protect him from the charge, but Lavinia has the proof that his alibi is false. It is written in her Bible,* along with her own and Coralee's eyewitness account of Marcus's whereabouts on the night of the massacre. Lavinia's knowledge buys her her freedom: she is not above a little blackmail herself, but in the cause of justice. Ben promises, in exchange for her information, to finance her school and take care of Coralee. And just in case he should change his mind, Lavinia keeps a tight hold on the Bible, the repository of the evidence. As she departs on her journey to her new life—not the insane asylum, but to do her

---

* That Bible has been too melodramatic for most critics to take seriously—but Hellman uses it ironically. Lavinia's particular "insanity" is supposed to be religious; religion put her in Marcus's power to have her declared insane. Now the Bible—her religion—has put him in Lavinia's power. Not only is the Bible too dirty a book for her black children to read, it is also the instrument of blackmail.

work in this world—she plays her own version of the Ophelia mad scene in *Hamlet*: to each of the others she gives a memento—a pin to Regina, her prayer book to Oscar, her father's watch to Ben, and her wedding ring (back) to Marcus. Of course they all want the Bible, but she is keeping that.

I have devoted this disproportionate amount of space to Lavinia because her character adds a new dimension to the Hubbard saga. She is neither a crazy woman nor a saintly one, although she has a touch of each, and her presence in the play means that some good blood has been brought into the Hubbard clan. That the character of Lavinia, modeled on Hellman's mother, as she tells us in the memoirs, should be the only bearer of good blood, is significant. It was Hellman's way of setting things to rights with the ghost of her own eccentric, misunderstood mother, who had been a source of irritation and embarrassment at times to her daughter.

After Lavinia's revelation, Ben becomes the tribal chief. He forces his father, to escape hanging, to sell him the family business for one dollar. He gives Birdie Bagtry a promised loan on Lionnet and insures that the plantation will come eventually to the Hubbards by clearing the way for Oscar to court Birdie. John Bagtry is out of the way, too, for the money will enable him to go to Brazil. Regina knows now where her bread is buttered. In the final moments of the play, Marcus, now stripped of power, goes to sit by his daughter:

MARCUS (*softly*): Pour me a cup of coffee, darling. *Regina looks at him, gets up, crosses to the table, pours coffee, brings it to him. Marcus pulls forward the chair next to him. Regina ignores the movement, crosses to chair near Ben, sits down.*

Curtain

Some critics applauded the play, others were not so kind, and reading it one can see why. The melodrama

(in the ordinary sense of the word) does get out of hand.
Hellman had an exchange on the subject with Brooks
Atkinson, who thought the play as a whole was a "witch's
brew of blackmail, insanity, cruelty, theft, torture, insult,
drunkenness, with a trace of incest thrown in for good
measure." But he congratulated her on some "scenes of
great theatrical intensity. . . ." and added, "What you
may find yourself wondering about is how an author
who overwrites a gaudy melodrama can write individual
scenes like Birdie's pathetic farewell in the second act
with such sure, piercing economy."[8] Hellman answered
him a short time later, at the invitation of the *Times*, but
mainly to the effect that since Atkinson didn't like action
or violence on the stage the two of them would never
agree. He would continue to "frown down" upon her, and
she would go on writing in her own way.[9]

But Hellman made a more enlightening comment on
the play in *Pentimento*. As she went into the past of the
Hubbards, she says,

I believed that I could now make clear that I had meant the
first play [*The Little Foxes*] as a kind of satire. I tried to
do that in *Another Part of the Forest*, but what I thought
funny or outrageous, the critics thought straight stuff; what
I thought was bite they thought sad, touching, or plotty and
melodramatic. Perhaps, as one critic said, I blow a stage to
pieces without knowing it.

Part, at least, of the satire was aimed at some dramatic forms as well as at the types of characters in this
play. The phrase, "another part of the forest," is, of
course, a commonplace stage direction in Renaissance
drama, including the plays of Shakespeare. One far-
fetched hypothesis is that Hellman may have been alluding
to the use of the phrase in *Titus Andronicus*,[10] an early
play of Shakespeare's in the exaggerated theatrical mode
of the tragedy of blood. Except for the names, Marcus
and Lavinia, there is no real evidence that Hellman meant

to refer to *Titus Andronicus*, but she certainly knew the genre and caught the spirit of it in both *The Little Foxes* and this play.

But there are further hints of satire and parody: Marcus is fond of the style Hellman calls "Greek Southern"—not only in architecture but in his taste for Aristotle and his other affectations; he sees himself as a sort of Marcus Aurelius—the beneficent Roman emperor called "the Philosopher." And if, as Hellman says, *The Little Foxes* was also intended to be satirical, then certainly one of the objects of the satire was Eugene O'Neill's trilogy, *Mourning Becomes Electra*, a civil-war tragedy in the Greek Freudian manner, modeled on the Greek *Oresteia* of Aeschylus. The Electra character there, morbidly attached first to her father, then her brother, is called Lavinia. In *Mourning Becomes Electra* Lavinia's mother is the Clytemnestra figure who kills her husband, a civil-war general, in a way so similar to the death of Horace at the hands of Regina, as to have been confusing critics (especially this one) ever since.[11]

But Hellman was also parodying herself and *The Little Foxes* in this play, and that may have caused the confusion and mixed reactions among critics. While she reiterates in the memoirs that she often makes fun of herself, the adjective most frequently used by others to describe Hellman is "formidable." One thinks twice before laughing at her, or determining whether or not she is laughing at herself. And she *did* direct *Another Part of the Forest* because she thought no one else could do it.

WATCH ON THE RHINE

Of *Watch on the Rhine*, Hellman said in *Pentimento*, "There are plays that, whatever their worth, come along at the right time, and the right time is the essence of the theater and the cinema." This instinct for timing, as well as for drama, has served her well in the plays, the memoirs, and her new film, *Julia*. But none of her works was ever more timely than *Watch on the Rhine*. It opened on April 1, 1941. The war in Europe, and the question of our imminent involvement, haunted the minds of Americans. Not only Poland and Czechoslovakia but now Holland, Norway, Belgium, and most of France had fallen to Hitler. Britain was undergoing the worst bombing of the war. In March Congress had passed the Lend-Lease Act permitting the president to send war material to those countries that were soon—after Pearl Harbor, on December 7 of that same year—to be our fighting allies.

If the play had not been concerned with such a deadly earnest theme, it might have been a comedy of manners. American and European characters are thrown together in order to say something about their differing values and customs—not only about good and evil. In looking back at her old diaries, Hellman was surprised to discover that she had had Henry James's two novels on this subject, *The American* and *The Europeans*, in the back of her mind at the time of writing *Watch on the Rhine*.

In construction, the first act is such a cliché of well-made drawing-room drama, as to be redeemed only by the wit and broad humor of the characterizations and actions. In the plush setting of a mansion in suburban Washington, one group of characters—including a black butler, French housekeeper, wealthy dowager "mistress of the house," and her son—are anxiously awaiting the arrival of another group of characters. In expressing anticipation and anxiety they provide the audience with details about the new arrivals. (This is the typical "exposition" of the well-made play.) When the guests arrive, we have a fine family "recognition scene" of the good people—after twenty years—full of happy surprises and further information. This is followed by an ominous scene of suspected recognition between two old enemies. The act concludes with evil just about to get the upper hand over good, before the intermission in which the audience can relish its suspense. This mechanical structure continues in the subsequent act, through a series of confrontations, crises, and resolutions between various characters, ending in a climactic confrontation and final dénouement. . . . catastrophic, but on a lofty note.

But the characterization in the play is interesting enough to overcome our awareness of its mechanical structure. The wealthy dowager, Fanny Farrelly, is the widow of a liberal judge and diplomat, to whose memory she constantly refers and whose portrait hangs on the living room wall throughout the play. Fanny has been an arbitrary dictator over her son, David, and would have been one also over her daughter, Sara, if Sara had not declared her independence twenty years before by marrying a German, Kurt Müller. Fanny, resisting all the way, will soon be educated and "liberalized" by Kurt and his children as the play progresses. As bossy as she is, Fanny's wit gives her charm. Part of her function in life is to find out the local gossip and improve on it—"wit it up"— and the rest is to keep her family in order, according to her own upperclass lights.

The primary story is that of the Müllers (spelled "Mueller" in earlier versions of the play). Kurt is an antifascist who has fought in Spain, as well as in Germany. He is not Jewish.

He is modeled on "Julia," as Hellman acknowledges in *Pentimento*, and in early manuscript drafts of the play (now in the Texas Collection) was a radical revolutionary socialist. Hellman dropped that complication in the final draft, with its suggestion that Kurt was a Communist, except for a few general comments about the inequalities of wealth and poverty. Kurt's family arrives hungry and ill-clothed at the Farrellys' mansion. Kurt carries the marks of torture by the fascists—scars and

broken hands. He has finally managed to bring his wife
and children to visit her mother and brother, where the
family can rest for a while. But Kurt himself is on a
mission—he is carrying $23,000 in cash, collected from
"the pennies of the poor who do not like Fascism." He
will soon have to leave his family in Washington and
take the money back to Europe, where it is needed to
free other anti-Nazi prisoners.

Staying with the Farrellys when the Müllers arrive
are a different group and breed of Europeans, Romanian
Count Teck de Brancovis and his wife Marthe. Teck is a
Nazi sympathizer and gambler—a professional Romanian aristocrat." (Hellman modeled him on a Romanian
Prince whom she had met and played poker with in
London in 1936.) Marthe has lived in Europe most of
her life and dislikes Nazis. The couple is visiting Fanny
because Marthe's mother and she were friends.

The marriage of Teck and Marthe has disintegrated.
They are in debt, living on credit. What little money they
have is being lost through Teck's gambling with his Nazi
friends at the German embassy in Washington. Marthe
is falling in love with David Farrelly, Fanny's thirty-nine
year old son, and is trying to find a way to leave her
husband. Kurt knows Teck's identity and his past, and
Teck is suspicious of Kurt's.

When the news breaks that three prominent anti-
fascists have been caught, imprisoned, and tortured by
the Nazis, Teck discovers that they are all close friends
of Kurt, and that he is a missing fourth on the Nazi's
wanted list. Teck threatens to turn Kurt in to the Nazi
embassy unless Kurt will give him $10,000 of the $23,000
he is carrying. Kurt refuses—the money is not his. Fanny
offers to give Teck $4,000 in cash, which she has in the
house, and a check for the remainder, dated a month in
advance, to give Kurt time to get back to Europe before
it is cashed. Kurt pretends to acquiesce in this blackmail,
but he knows that it is a trap: Teck will betray him and

his imprisoned friends anyway, in exchange for a hard-to-get German visa. When Fanny leaves the room to get the money, Kurt faces Teck with this knowledge. Before Teck can answer, Kurt attacks him and knocks him unconscious. With gun in hand, Kurt carries Teck out to the garden, where he shoots him.

Sara knows what is happening and that it is inevitable. She calls the airline and reserves a seat for Kurt, under another name, on the next plane to Texas, where he will cross over to Mexico and then to Europe. When Kurt returns from the garden, they explain to Fanny and David, who come to understand that Kurt has done what he had to do. The killing of Teck was an act of war, except that "when you kill in a war, it is not so lonely." Kurt will take Teck's body in the car with him, and leave it there when he hides the car. After two days the family will report the two of them missing. By that time Kurt will have escaped.

Fanny and David give Kurt their support. The children and Sara will stay with them there, with little hope that Kurt will ever return. There is a touching farewell scene; Kurt leaves, and Sara goes upstairs to comfort the children. Fanny and David prepare to face what trouble may come. Fanny says, "Well, here we are. We are shaken out of the magnolias, eh?" Hellman said in *Pentimento* that this was her purpose—"to write a play about nice, liberal Americans whose lives would be shaken up by Europeans, by a world the new Fascists had won because the old values had long been dead." In the play, Fanny and David see those old values of culture, honor, and dignity in Kurt.

Quantitatively, there is more comic and romantic byplay in *Watch on the Rhine* than there is tense melodrama. The children provide some of the comedy in their relationship with their gruff, basically sentimental, grandmother. The warmth between members of the Müller family, and the budding romance (we never quite see it

flower) between Marthe and David give the audience
hope that youth—or romantic middle age—and love will
prevail over decadence and hate. This comedy of manners
fills most of the first two acts; in spite of its "well-made"
devices, the play is not tightly constructed. Some critics
thought the first half dragged or consisted of over-
emotional padding, but most described it as "pleasantly
discursive" or "spontaneous" and witty. Most agreed that,
melodramatic or not, the characters and the European-
American contrast were skillfully drawn.

   Watch on the Rhine won the New York Drama Critics
Circle Award for 1941. This was no small honor, for the
major playwrights of the day all had war dramas running
concurrently, or almost so, with *Watch on the Rhine.*
(These included Maxwell Anderson's *Key Largo*, Ernest
Hemingway's *Fifth Column*, Robert Sherwood's *There
Shall Be No Night*, Elmer Rice's *Flight to the West*, Philip
Barry's *Liberty Jones*, S. N. Behrman's *The Talley
Method*, and F. H. Brennan's *The Wookey*.) The most
often cited was Sherwood's, but most critics agreed that
Sherwood depended somewhat too heavily on sermonizing.
As Wolcott Gibbs said (and he was not always kind to
Hellman) ". . . for the first time, as far as I am concerned
(and I'm not forgetting *There Shall Be No Night*) the
fundamental issue of our time has been treated with the
dignity, insight, and sound theatrical intelligence that it
demands."[12]

   Hellman's activities on behalf of antifascist causes
were in the limelight at this time, especially her money-
raising efforts for the Joint Anti-Fascist Refugee Committee. This fact was not lost on some of the critics, both
of the right and the left. She was both praised and damned
by the communist press. In general, they praised her for
being antifascist, but thought she should have been more
positively procommunist. Some conservatives thought she
should have called the play anti-Nazi instead of anti-

Fascist, unless she meant it to be interpreted as pro-Communist.

Hellman had taken voluminous notes on the history and background of events in Europe to prepare herself to write *Watch on the Rhine*. In addition to the notebooks and drafts of the play now to be found in the University of Texas Collection, Hellman made 400 to 500 more pages of factual notes—typewritten, single-spaced.[13] She must have drawn on this material for her next play about the war and American wartime attitudes—*The Searching Wind*.

4

Bystanders

THE SEARCHING WIND

Like *Watch on the Rhine*, *The Searching Wind* sets off
the microcosm of manners against the macrocosm of world
events. When the two worlds impinged on each other in
Watch on the Rhine, liberal upperclass Americans were
"shaken out of the magnolias." In *The Searching Wind*,
the magnolias are shaking, but the liberals hardly notice
until too late. *Watch on the Rhine* was a play about action in crisis. This is a play about the inaction of bystanders, a cardinal sin in Hellman's morality. The inaction takes the form of appeasement and compromises, in
love and war—in the private and the public world.

The play was baffling to many of the audiences; an
explanation of the title might have helped. It was a quotation from Hellman's black cook and housekeeper, Helen,
and is explained in *An Unfinished Woman*—"It takes a
searching wind to find the tree you sit in." The sentence
means, in effect, "Who can tell what side you are on if
you don't know your own mind?" In the memoir the
sentence applied to upperclass liberal attitudes toward
racism, which to Helen seemed confused and unformu-
lated. In these two war plays, some well-meaning, affluent
Americans were shaken out of the manorial tree by the
events of World War II—but the searching wind could
not even find the tree that many others sat in.

In this play a "liberal" turns out to be one who cannot believe in villainy, and who in the name of caution, and keeping an open mind, made compromises with evil— i.e., with fascism, at the cost of lives of future generations. Three scenes take place in the present—1944—the year in which the action begins and ends. Three scenes take place in the past—1922, 1923, 1938. The flashbacks represent three political and personal crises in the lives of the three major characters. These are Alex Hazen, a career diplomat; his wealthy wife, Emily; and "the other woman," Catherine (Cassie) Bowman. At each crisis, Alex appeases the fascists, and his wife appeases her rival—her ex-best friend. Alex tries to appease both women, and to keep them both.

Outside the trio (as commentators on the action) are the old man—Moses Taney, Emily's father—and the young man—his grandson, Sam Hazen. Hellman often uses this arrangement of characters along an age spectrum —the old at one end, the young at the other, affecting or commenting on the action of the characters in between; e.g., Mary and Mrs. Tilford in *The Children's Hour*, Fanny and Bodo in *Watch on the Rhine*, Mrs. Ellis and Sophie in *The Autumn Garden*. Moses (who might have led the children of Israel to freedom, but did not) is a charming but disillusioned fighting liberal, retired editor of a once great newspaper. He has withdrawn from political decision-making himself, but comments bitterly on other people's diplomatic compromises. The grandson, Sam, is one of Hellman's soldier-boys who has finally found a purposeful life in the army, only to lose his best friend, his respect for his parents, and his ability to make war in the process.

The framework of present time opens and closes with the conflict between Emily Hazen and Cas Bowman. Hellman created curiosity, and no small amount of befuddlement, in her audience by having Emily invite Cas to hers and Alex's home in Washington—nobody knows why.

Then, through the subsequent flashbacks into the past we are still unsure, until in the final scene, at the house a few hours after scene one, we learn Emily's purpose. Let us look at the flashbacks as a series of double crisis-confrontations.

Crisis one. 1922. Moses, his daughter Emily, and her best friend, Cas, along with the Taney maid, Sophronia, are visiting in Rome, where Alex Hazen is a young diplomat in the American embassy. Mussolini is marching on Rome, and Cassie is marching on Alex, whom Emily expects to marry. Mussolini takes over. Alex agrees with his boss, the American ambassador, that open opposition to the fascists would be intervention in Italian internal affairs. His failure to take a strong political stand precipitates a quarrel with Cassie. Though this is not known to Emily they have been lovers and have thought of marriage. Now Cassie decides to return to her teaching job in America for a year to think it over. Emily's response to Cas and her challenge is that of passive resistance— to stay in Rome where Alex is. (It works, and she catches him.)

Crisis two. Berlin, 1923. It is the time of the first organized antisemitic riots. Emily is married to Alex, and Cas has made it a habit to follow them (and to see Alex) when she is on vacation in Europe. The scene takes place in a Berlin restaurant where Alex is waiting for Emily, and (unknowingly) being watched by Cas at another table. The noises of riot and threats against Jews are heard outside the restaurant. Emily comes in shocked by the spectacle she has just witnessed of German ex-soldiers beating up old Jews. Alex's response to the crisis is to calm down the people in the restaurant and to blame the riot on the negligence of the police. He is refusing to face the complicity of the police in the antisemitism.*

---

* In an earlier draft of the play, Hellman had included another character, a German captain of the Freikorps, an illegal fascist

Emily sees Cas and is polite. Cas takes the offensive and accuses Emily of having stolen Alex from her. Emily claims not guilty—Cas and Alex had already quarreled. Emily offers friendship—reconciliation, appeasement.

Crisis three. The third double confrontation takes place in Paris in 1938, when the Munich agreement— the archexample of appeasement of Hitler by Britain and France—is about to take place. Alex must send his recommendation to the United States government. Again, he refuses to believe in evil and corruption, even when a Nazi attempts to pressure him into trying to keep France and Britain out of war with Germany. He holds out hope that Hitler may keep his promise not to annex more territory after the Sudetenland, and supports Chamberlain's efforts to keep "peace in our time."

Emily also wants peace at any price, now in politics as well as love. She does not want to send her son to war. She and Alex quarrel—then make peace—about her hobnobbing with pro-Nazi European socialites, including the banker with whom she has deposited some of her money. (The money is a sore point with Alex, who does not like to think of himself as rich or as subject to the influences of wealth and position.)

But Cas, at Emily's invitation, has been to see Alex. Before Emily arrives, they have arranged a rendezvous. Alex has decided that he loves Emily but is "in love with" Cas. When Emily comes, she tells Alex that as she entered she saw Cas in the lobby, but was afraid to confront her. And thus, she leaves Alex in the hands of the enemy, as Chamberlain—and Alex—left Europe.

In the last scene, which takes up the 1944 action again, Hellman brings all the confrontations together, the women, the war, the generations. It turns out that

army of ex-soldiers. He challenges Alex, and Alex throws him out of the restaurant. Hellman dropped this scene, probably because it showed Alex in too belligerent a light.[1]

Emily had invited Cas to the house in act one in order to have it out with her once and for all, to accuse her directly of husband-stealing. Now Cas breaks down and tells Emily that the accusation is true: she had been out to get Alex away from Emily and to punish Emily for marrying him. Alex agrees to let Cas go—without a struggle, and he relaxes with his wife.

The major confrontation, however, is between Sam and his elders. This, too, has been hanging fire since the opening scene. We learned there that Sam had been wounded; now we find he must lose his leg. In spite of his grandfather's efforts to educate him, Sam is not an intellectual—he trusts action and sincere human relations, not words. He had felt at home in the army with fighting men, and especially with his friend, Leck, who was killed in the same battle in which Sam was wounded. His war experiences have made him ashamed of his family of "bystanders" and now he tells them why.

He is ashamed of his grandfather, the great liberal, who now just sits back and watches; of his father who went along with Munich; and of his mother with her rich pro-Nazi friends. Then with an almost apologetic patriotism, Sam accuses his parents of damaging the country which he loves:

> "I don't want any more of Father's mistakes, for any reason, good or bad, or yours, Mother, because I think they do [the country] harm. . . . I am ashamed of both of you, and that's the truth. . . . I don't like losing my leg . . . but everybody's welcome to it as long as it means a little something and helps to bring us out someplace. All right. I've said enough. Let's have a drink."

The public did not seem to be troubled by the implied impotence in that speech, and its final "let's have a drink." The play ran for 318 performances, almost as long as *Watch on the Rhine*. Most people could respond to Sam's commitment to his country, unlike his father's vacillation, signified by his sacrifice in the service. But a brave gesture and denunciation of his elders hardly provides a solution to the problem those elders faced.

The critics, on the whole, were not kind to the play. They had good reason. Neither the theme, nor the plot structure, nor the characters ever came completely clear on the stage—and they take considerable analyzing even on the printed page. The theme of compromise was simplistic; some critics thought Hellman was too hard on Hazen. One questioned why she believed that there was "a moral difference. . . . between Chamberlain's attempt to turn Hitler East and Stalin's attempt to turn him West."[2]

Most critics thought the love triangle silly and trivial—not worth all the mystery about it—and I tend to agree. The characters of the women are never clear—that's part of the mystery: which is the bad one? Cas is intelligent, and idealistic in her insistence that Alex take a firm stand: John Gassner called her "high-minded,"[3] but her actions are certainly not high-minded as she herself confesses. But since the obscurity of the play may partly be the result of private images and allusions, such as the title, the clue to Cas Bowman's character may be in her last name. In the memoirs Bowman is the name of some wealthy cousins whom Hellman disliked. (Sophronia, the name of Hellman's black nurse in New Orleans also appears in the play, and no doubt there are other significant names.)

In the 1960s Hellman told an interviewer that she hated "theme" plays. She apparently decided to abandon them after this one—if not in adaptations, at least in her original work. Her political activity in liberal or left-wing causes became separate from her playwriting. *Another Part of the Forest* followed *The Searching Wind.* Then came an adaptation from the French of Emmanuel Roblès, *Montserrat*, another play about compromise and the heroism of those who are willing to die for their convictions. But Hellman's next original play, *The Autumn Garden*, concerned itself with individual persons, bystanders who try to come to terms with what they have made, or failed to make, of their own private lives.

THE AUTUMN GARDEN

It is customary for critics of Hellman's later plays to call them Chekhovian, and to distinguish between the realism of Ibsen and that of Chekhov. Any direct influence of Chekhov on Hellman is hard to ascertain—her edition of Chekhov's letters was not published until four years after *The Autumn Garden* was completed. But "influence" or not, the distinction between Ibsen and Chekhov is interesting because it roughly parallels that between the "despoiler" and the "bystander" plays.

Ibsen's realistic plays are strongly plotted around an idea or social problem. His characters oppose or react to each other in a series of confrontations, building toward a climax.

Chekhov, on the other hand, emphasizes mood, not plot. As a critic of *The Autumn Garden* said, "He did not reveal his people. He invited them to be self-revealing. Their plight did not raise ethical questions. His characters were victims of themselves; wandering egos, frustrated and despairing, who lived in a constant state of spiritual cross-ventilation. . . ."[4]

Any summation of the "plot" of *The Autumn Garden* is a summation of the characters, those slightly faded flowers clustering together for protection in a boarding house—a summer resort, modeled on one Hellman had visited. It is also reminiscent of the boarding house that had been run by her aunts, Hannah and Jenny. (In an early draft of the play, two sisters were the innkeepers.)

Hellman, unlike Chekhov, has more scorn than pity

for these passive characters. The only two in the play who
have any vitality are a tough-minded old woman who will
never wither until she dies, and an equally tough young
girl, who knows what she wants and gets it when she
hears the loud knock of opportunity.

When the curtain rises, representatives of all the
major clusters, except one, are on stage. Of course, they
are waiting for the missing set to arrive. At the Tuckerman house now are Constance Tuckerman, the owner, a
plucky but romantic southern lady who was left impover-
ished by her supposedly wealthy parents, and converted
the family summer home into the boardinghouse. One of
her most faithful summer boarders is Edward Crossman,
a middle-aged intellectual who was once in love with
Constance, and who now finds his chief solace in alcohol.
Constance has a young niece, Sophie, daughter of her
brother and his French wife. Sophie's father died during
the war and Constance thought it her duty to rescue
Sophie from poverty in a French village. Now Sophie
helps her aunt with the work at the boardinghouse.

Sophie is engaged to Frederick Ellis, a young man
who is staying at the Tuckerman house with his grandmother and his mother. The grandmother, Mrs. Mary
Ellis, holds the family purse strings and knows the power
of her wealth. She dominates her daughter, Carrie, who
in turn dominates her son, Frederick. The engagement of
Frederick and Sophie is acknowledged between them to be
a matter of convenience. Frederick will give Sophie financial security, and she will give him a home and respec-
tability. Carrie approves since she feels instinctively that
Sophie is no rival. Frederick's real emotional interest,
however, is in Payson, a male writer whose work he is
editing, and who has a dubious reputation. Some critics
have called Frederick a "passive-dependent" mother's boy,
who is latently homosexual. But nobody in the play, except possibly his mother, considers the inclination to be
latent. The Ellises—Grandmother, Mother, and Frederick

—are planning a trip to Europe, without Sophie. Frederick is determined to invite Payson to go as his guest.

The other regular summer boarders are General Benjamin Griggs and his wife, Rose. Rose is a comic character, pathetic but childish and silly. Her husband wants a divorce, and plans to leave her whether she divorces him or not. Griggs has his own Oedipal hangups: he had always wanted love from a serious woman like his mother. To get even, Rose boasts of a love affair she had when the general was away during the war. But Griggs is beyond caring; he just wants out.

Into this garden comes the serpent, Nick—the old Nick—Denery and his rich ninny of a wife, Nina.* Nick is to be the *deus* (or *diabolus*) *ex machina* whose meddling in the lives of others "shakes them out of their magnolias." He goes from group to group making trouble. His only motive is to display his charm and use his power to manipulate others. He flirts with all the women, but when they begin to respond, protects himself against any commitment. He has been doing this for years to his wife who sees through it, is sick of his meddling and philandering, but cannot make up her mind to leave him.

Nick's first victim is Constance Tuckerman, who was once so in love with him that she rejected Ned Crossman. Twenty-three years before, Nick, an artist of sorts, had painted Constance's portrait. Now he cruelly persuades her to let him paint her again. His plan is to retrieve from her the original portrait and exhibit the two together. Nick dresses Constance in rags, and in the portrait, paints her as a sad, povertystricken old woman. (A reading of Henry James's short story, "The Liar," reveals some inter-

* The name, Denery, appeared in *An Unfinished Woman*, attached to a boy who had hit Lillian (about age 12) in a tug of war, and whom she repaid by a blow on the head with a porcelain coffeepot. There are other suggested connections between characters from the memoirs and those in *The Autumn Garden*, but they will have to be identified by future Hellman biographers.

esting parallels.) All the time he keeps up a lie to Constance that he, Nick, really loved her when he married Nina, and still does, but that Ned Crossman still loves her too and wants to marry her. Nick will not allow Constance to look at the new portrait of herself; now he encourages her to fantasize about Crossman.

Nick then turns his beneficent attention to the Ellises. He informs Carrie that he had seen Fred in the travel agency, booking passage to Europe for Payson. Nick warns Carrie that Payson was involved in "a filthy little scandal in Rome." Carrie thanks him for the information (which could be false scandal-mongering) and faces Frederick with it. He still insists on taking Payson with him. But his grandmother forces Carrie to tell Frederick that he can leave on the trip with Payson, but must "make clear to his guest that his ten thousand a year ends today and will not begin again." The threat works. Payson backs out of the trip if he has to pay his own way. Frederick is heartbroken.

Nick's wife, Nina, has been through this type of thing often before. He can never leave things alone. She says to him, "I can smell it: it's all around us. The flower-like odor right before it becomes faded and heavy. It travels ahead of you, Nick, whenever you get most helpful, most loving, and most lovable." And she threatens to leave him as she has done before.

Nick has tampered also with the Griggs's marriage. He comforts Rose by flirting with her. For his trouble he gains her confidence and the promise of a $5000 commission to paint a portrait of her homely niece. Rose is ill, is beginning to feel amorous toward Nick, and asks for his advice. He suggests that she go to a doctor—not to be cured, but to be certified that she is truly ill so that her husband will not leave her.

It is Nick's philandering, plus alcohol, that brings the plot to a climax, and the characters to their senses. Nick has been drinking throughout act two. He makes

advances to Sophie, who is trying to get to sleep on the
living-room sofa, then passes out on the couch before
anything can happen. Sophie simply leaves him there
and spends the night in a chair across the room. There
is an uproar when the two are discovered by Mrs. Ellis
and others in the morning. Hellman works hard to convince us that this is a catastrophe. Everyone in that little
town will hear the gossip and think that Nick has seduced
Sophie. Sophie makes use of her advantage, and in so
doing, indirectly returns all the others to the reality of
their situations.

Nick, himself, is out of the action. Now that he is in
disgrace, Nina comes back to him and the truth about
her is revealed. She needs to punish and be punished.
Nick tells her, "You needed to look down on me, darling.
. . . You like to—demean yourself." (In *An Unfinished
Woman*, Hellman gives this characteristic to Dorothy
Parker.)

The Ellises try to persuade Sophie to go to Europe
with them, but she refuses. Frederick has stopped moping
about Payson, but Sophie knows, as does old Mrs. Ellis,
that Frederick will always be his mother's boy. Sophie also
knows that she must have another source of income now.
From Nina she demands $5000. Otherwise she will spread
the word that Nick seduced her. With the money she will
be free to go back to Europe to help her mother.

Nick was right about Rose and Ben Griggs. When
Ben knows that she is ill, he gives in to Rose's appeal
that he take care of her. For Ben escape is not possible;
it is too late. His speech of self-insight was written by
Dashiell Hammett, and Hellman said that it summarized
the philosophy of the play. (And it does sound like what
John Mason Brown called the "spiritual cross-ventilation"
of Chekhov's characters.)

"There are no big moments you can reach unless you've
a pile of smaller moments to stand on. That big hour of

decision, the turning point in your life, the someday you've counted on when you'd suddenly wipe out your past mistakes, do the work you'd never done, think the way you'd never thought, have what you'd never had—it just doesn't come suddenly. You've trained yourself for it while you waited—or you've let it all run past you and frittered yourself away. I've frittered myself away, Crossman."

Now it is Ned Crossman's and Constance's turn for self-knowledge. Ned faces the fact that he has wasted himself—has become a drunk, living in a room and passing the day until night when the bars open. This is not because Constance turned him down, as he once persuaded himself, but because he "wanted it that way."

Constance has decided that she wasted herself, too, waiting for Nick when she really wanted Ned Crossman all the time. She asks him to marry her but it is too late. He is sorry that he had deluded her and himself into thinking he was in love with her. The curtain falls on his declaration:

CROSSMAN: . . . Sorry I fooled you and sorry I fooled myself. And I've never liked liars—least of all those who lie to themselves.

CONSTANCE: Never mind. Most of us lie to ourselves. Never mind.

The only two characters in the play who have not lied to themselves are the young and old realists who have acknowledged the value of money, Sophie and Mrs. Ellis. Sophie is building her future by taking action in the present; the old lady built a triumphant past in the same way.

The Autumn Garden had mixed reviews and ran for 102 performances. It was revived in the winter of 1976 at the Long Wharf Theater in New Haven, Connecticut. Walter Kerr, who had some faults to find with the original production, was fulsome in his praise of this

one. He pointed out that the emphasis had changed somewhat in the two productions. In 1951 Sophie's blackmail
had seemed melodramatic, but in the new production it
becomes (as it is in the script) a way for Sophie to keep
her dignity. She will not accept charity. She insists that
she be credited with blackmail.

A few critics, especially among literary scholars,
have seen optimism and compassion in this play. As for
the optimism, Hellman said in a newspaper interview
that the characters in the play led empty lives, but that
"the play isn't meant to say that people can't do anything about such emptiness. It is meant to say the opposite—they can do a great deal with their lives."[5]
That is, if they start soon enough. But she emphasized
that at middle age "if you have wasted what you had in
you, it is too late to do much about it."[6] So one can be
optimistic about life if one is *not* like the people in the
play; if one takes hold of some clear commitment and
works toward it.

The problems of the characters in *The Autumn
Garden* are individual and personal. There is no cosmic
background of war or politics, no ethical decisions to
make as in *The Searching Wind*. The concerns of these
people are all of the kind that Cassie Bowman called
"frivolous," and Hellman seems to agree with her. Harold
Clurman, who directed the original *Autumn Garden*,
speaks of Hellman's "feelings about most of us of the
educated near-upper class. We are earnest, we yearn, but
we are not serious, we have no clear purpose. We have
no binding commitments to ourselves or to others; we
are attached to nothing."[7] And Clurman added that Hellman's attitude toward her characters was almost cruel
compared to Chekhov's feeling for his. "The blunderers
in Chekhov are brothers in our nobility even as in our
abjectness. The characters in *The Autumn Garden* are
our equals only in what we do not respect about ourselves."[8]

Hellman has always been a doer—impatient with thinkers or perceivers or flounderers. Her old anger against evil and injustice in the early plays seems now to have become a general irritability and petulance toward human inadequacy. She deplores failure through lack of direction, self-discipline, or energy—"wasting time." At the end of *An Unfinished Woman* she explains what she meant by the title: "All I mean is that I left too much of me unfinished because I wasted too much time. However. . . ." Most readers, of course, thought what Hellman wanted them to—if *she* wasted time, how about me? In any case, the time-wasting characters of these two plays, *The Searching Wind* and *The Autumn Garden*, have been given their implied "however" too, but that is the extent of Hellman's compassion.

In the years between *The Autumn Garden*, 1951, and her next and last original play, *Toys in the Attic*, 1960, Hellman tried her hand at adaptations[9] of plays in a less realistic mode than her own. These were difficult years for her—the House Un-American Activities Committee hearings, Hammett's jail sentence and subsequent illness and decline, the loss of the farm, the Hollywood blacklisting. In 1954 she edited the collection of Chekhov's letters.[10] Her introductory essay and the three brief prefaces to groups of the letters are warmly admiring of the Russian dramatist.

Hellman's adaptation of *The Lark*, a play about Joan of Arc by the French playwright, Jean Anouilh, was completed and performed in 1955. *The Lark* had been translated by the British poet-playwright Christopher Fry and performed in London earlier that same year with moderate success. Fry's version was more literary and philosophical than it was dramatic. Hellman worked with other translations, tightened the action, simplified the language, and turned the play into exciting theater, with a first-rate part for Julie Harris as Joan. Like *Montserrat*, the play appealed to Hellman's love of a good fight and her admiration of the honorable professional soldier. She saw Joan more as a modern career woman than as either saint or peasant. *The Lark* was Hellman's most successful adaptation; it ran for 229 performances.

The following year saw the production of *Candide*, subtitled "a comic operetta based upon Voltaire's satire." Hellman wrote the book for this elaborate musical; Leonard Bernstein did the music and Richard Wilbur, a talented and distinguished poet, wrote the lyrics. Other geniuses who had a hand in the production were John Latouche, Dorothy Parker, and the director, Tyrone Guthrie. Hellman spent a year of hard work on *Candide*, testified to by the many manuscripts, including twelve complete versions, in the University of Texas library. Ultimately, however, there were too many chefs to produce a *chef d'oeuvre*. Hellman's narrative line gradually diminished in importance, but when *Candide* closed after seventy-three performances, and nobody could fault the music, lyrics, dancing, etc., they blamed the failure on what was left of Hellman's book.

If musical comedy was alien to Hellman's talent, so was her final adaptation. It was an off-beat, zany, satirical comedy about middle-class Jews, called *My Mother, My Father, and Me*, and based on the novel, *How Much?* by Burt Blechman.[11] The play failed, but before the fiasco, Hellman had already begun to draw on her own life for materials, rather than on other people's work. By 1960 the imaginative use of memory, which was eventually to lead to her second career, had contributed to the success of *Toys in the Attic*.

TOYS IN THE ATTIC

Toys in the Attic is Hellman's last original play to date and her most textured and complex. The texture is not simply a result of intricate plotting, but of many-layered, often ambiguous characterization. Still, the play is less Chekhovian than *The Autumn Garden*, and more like the old Hellman, full of mystery and melodrama.* The characters muddle their way toward a kind of self-insight, like those in *The Autumn Garden*, but the truth about them turns out to be bizarre and the plot ends with a violent climax. In contrast to Hellman's active villains like the Hubbards or heroes like Kurt Müller, these characters are what I have called bystanders. They do not intend evil or opposition to evil; they are hungry only for love, and their need for it, sometimes confused with the need for money, accomplishes their fate.

The idea for the play had been suggested to Hellman by Dashiell Hammett, as she tells us in *Pentimento*. The play was to center on a man—"Other people, people who say they love him, want him to make good, be rich." He does, and then discovers that they really don't like him rich. He thwarts his own success and ends up worse than he was at the start. Hellman tried to develop the idea, but found that she could do it only if she could write it about the women around such a man—the people who thought they wanted him to succeed but actually needed him to fail.

The man in question is Julian Berniers, thirty-four, a good-looking ne'er-do-well who has been raised by his two doting older sisters, Anna and Carrie, in the family house in New Orleans. After several business failures, Julian marries Lily Prine, a rich young girl whose mother, Albertine Prine, has given them $10,000 as a wedding present. The couple moves to Chicago, and Julian invests the money in a shoe factory, which, like his previous

---

* One critic, Jacob H. Adler, alleged that Miss Hellman had modeled the characters in *Toys in the Attic* on those in Chekhov's *Three Sisters*.[12] According to Moody, however, Miss Hellman said that the idea "had never crossed her mind."[13]

ventures, fails. But he returns to New Orleans mysteriously
wealthy, carrying $150,000 on his person. He and Lily
arrive at the sisters' home laden with gifts. Julian is now
in command; he has bought his sisters the things that he
and they always thought they wanted: tickets to Europe,
fancy clothes, a new piano, a new refrigerator, and a deed
to the house. (He has paid the mortgage.) Julian has
even taken it upon himself to write letters of resignation
to his sisters' employers. (There is something of the meddling do-gooder in him, like Nick Denery of *The Autumn
Garden*—another weak man married to a rich wife.)

Julian's money, with his new independence, threatens
to undermine the lives of all the women who claim to
love him. His two sisters had complained of their lot, but
now that they can sell the house that they have always
hated, and travel, as they have always wanted, they feel
lost. Anna, the more sensible and honest of the two, faces
the fact that they have always lived for Julian, have always needed him to be dependent upon them. She has
seen also that Carrie's possessiveness of Julian has masked
an incestuous longing for him.

Lily, Julian's wife, adores him, but her love is also
destructive, of both Julian and herself. She is a child,
chronologically twenty-one, but mentally and emotionally
about twelve. She is torn between satisfaction in the
knowledge that her money had originally made Julian
dependent on her, and fear that he might have wanted
only her money. The thought that her mother might have
sold her to Julian to get rid of her is intolerable, second
only to her fear of losing him. Lily is in a state of near-
hysteria throughout the play, never knowing where she
stands with either her mother or her husband. Her terror
and her fanatical attempt to discover what she calls
"truth" accidentally bring about the catastrophe at the
end of the play.

Although Albertine, Lily's mother, has always found
her daughter a nuisance, she did not pay Julian to marry

her—he was in love with Lily. Hellman explained Albertine in an interview, while she was still in the process of
writing the play: "She's a very rich lady. She's always
wanted to get rid of her daughter. . . . So the marriage
has delighted her, and she's the only one who feels sort
of sorry for this poor bastard [Julian] and she'd like to
see him keep the money and keep the girl for that matter,
too."[14] Albertine's lover is her mulatto chauffeur, Henry
Simpson, whom Lily hates as a rival for her mother's
affection. Henry understands the situation, and does what
he can to help the mother and daughter communicate.

Most of acts one and two are taken up with unanswered questions to keep the audience guessing: Why
do the characters behave as they do? Who is a mysterious
woman whom Julian has been seeing, and who calls him
at the house? Where did Julian's wealth come from? The
end of act two provides most of the answers. Julian made
the money in a real-estate deal financed by his ex-mistress,
Charlotte Warkins, the "mystery woman." He had been
her lover long ago, and now they are friends. Charlotte
needs money to escape from the husband she has long
hated. She has put up the cash for Julian to buy two
cheap parcels of swampland, which she knew would be
indispensable to her husband, Cyrus, in a business ven-
ture. When the play opens, Julian has sold him the lots
for the hold-up price of $150,000, a share of which will
go to Charlotte. We discover that Charlotte is part black,
a fact unknown to her husband.

The knowledge of Julian's past sexual relationship
with Charlotte Warkins throws Carrie into a frenzy, and
heightens Lily's hysteria. Carrie's feelings turn into hatred
for her sister when Anna makes Carrie face the truth of
her incestuous love for Julian: "You want to sleep with
him and always have." Lily's wild jealousy is intensified
by the fact that Julian has been impotent since they have
been in his sisters' house. Whatever the clinical cause—
the emasculating presence of his sisters in the house, or

as Anna alleges, his unconscious awareness of Carrie's
tabooed "lust"—Julian thinks of the condition as temporary. He loves Lily, who had never threatened his man-
hood, and thinks that all will be well when he and Lily
have gone away together, the house has been sold, and his
sisters dispatched abroad. He goes happily off to wind up
the transaction—to meet Charlotte and give her her share
of the money.

The women left behind are apprehensive—Lily that
Julian may not come back to her at all, and Carrie that
he will leave with Lily. Anna has determined that she will
go to Europe without Carrie, and makes her exit to pack.
(This is the most vital exit in the play. Without it the
catastrophe could not take place.) In the tense scene that
follows, Carrie satisfies her jealousy by allowing Lily to
believe—without actually saying so—that Julian married
her for her money and will now leave her for Charlotte.
With pathetic, childlike reasoning, Lily decides to beg
Charlotte to give her one more year with Julian, and if
he still loves Charlotte after that she can have him. Carrie
stands by while Lily telephones Cyrus Warkins to ask
him to give her message to Charlotte. Lily reveals the
whole story, including the fact that Charlotte is of mixed
blood. Carrie is silent, except to supply the crucial information that Julian and Charlotte are now meeting at
Sailor's Lane near the depot. Warkins sends his men
there, and they beat and slash the couple.

Julian limps home in a state of collapse. All his new-
found confidence is gone: he cannot understand how he
could have "assed up" this simple deal. Lily's mother
finally listens to her when Lily confesses, "Mama, I did it."
Albertine—still sympathetic to Julian—begs Lily to keep
the secret to herself, not to "kill him with the truth."
Julian seems defeated now, for good, even when he says,
"Got to start again." The sisters hover over him; Carrie
is now the smiling decision-maker, the boss, even though
Anna—apparently—will stay. The child bride stays, too,

with a promise from Albertine that if Julian discovers the truth, Lily can always go home to mother.

I have given only the bare bones of the plot and the barest sketch of the characters, whom Hellman identifies with many interesting "tags": Anna has headaches, Carrie likes to visit the cemetery, Lily walks around in her underwear and speaks a kind of inarticulate baby-talk. The really complex action of the play is not so much in the plot, as in the shifting relationships between the characters, and the morality—or lack of it—that seems to guide them. The destruction of Julian is accomplished in the name of "love," but that love represents a compulsion that neither Carrie nor Lily can control, and that Anna, finally, cannot resist or escape. Carrie, of course, knew exactly what she was doing when she let Lily make that telephone call; the defeated Julian and Lily would henceforth be in Carrie's power. Nevertheless, she too is a victim. Alan S. Downer, critic and historian of the stage, put it this way: "She is what evil must always be, the other side of good, tragic because she cannot know of her enslavement, because she can never have the opportunity to escape."[15]

Hellman places the burden of evil on Lily, as well as on Carrie, just as she does on all of the moral weaklings in her plays, and later, the memoirs. Her judgment is summed up in the speech that Albertine calls her "goodbye present" to Lily: "The pure and the innocent often bring harm to themselves and those they love and, when they do, for some reason that I do not know, the injury is very great."

To a theater audience, as to a first-time reader, the characters in *Toys in the Attic* keep about them an air of mystery as, no doubt, Hellman intended. Some of the mystery can be cleared up, however, by reading the early drafts of the play, and by relating these to the materials now available in Hellman's memoirs. This is *not* to say that any character, or group of characters, in the play is drawn literally from life, or that the memoirs "tell all." But some puzzles are clarified, particularly that of the relationship between the two sisters, and of the peculiar behavior of Lily and her relationship to her mother.

In the play, the older of the two sisters, Anna, is the more intelligent, the more independent and humorous. Carrie, the younger, is prettier and more feminine—in a fluttery way—but she takes control in the end. The two women appear to the reader or audience to be entirely different, but in the play, Albertine says that she confuses them: "Strange. Sometimes I can't tell which of you is speaking. . . . It is as if you had exchanged faces, back and forth, back and forth."

In an early draft of the play Anna had been called Hannah. Any reader of the memoirs will see a superficial resemblance—without hint of abnormality, however —between Hellman's two aunts and her father, and the sisters and Julian. The two aunts seem clearly differentiated from each other in the memoirs; but Hellman noticed in them their similarity, as well as the same inexplicable turnabout in supremacy that takes place between Anna and Carrie. In *Pentimento*, there is this revealing paragraph:

I suppose all women living together take on what we think of as male and female roles, but my aunts had made a rather puzzling mix-about. Jenny, who was the prettier, the softer in face and manner, had assumed a confidence she didn't have, and had taken on, demanded, I think, the practical, less pleasant duties. Hannah, who had once upon a time been more intelligent than Jenny, had somewhere given over, and although she held the official job. . . . it was Jenny who called the tunes for their life together. I don't think this changeabout of roles ever fooled my father, or that he paid much attention to it, but then he had grown up with them and knew about whatever it was that happened to their lives.

Toys in the Attic plays imaginatively with the notion of what *might* have happened to similar lives.

The memoirs contain other hints about characters and situations in *Toys*—after all, many of them started out as toys in Hellman's own attic. Sometimes, she said, they appeared in the plays without her conscious knowledge: she had not realized, for example, until it was pointed out to her, that her great-aunt Lily, whose mulatto chauffeur had been her lover, had provided the "seed" of the character of Albertine Prine. Hellman's surprise at this realization may sound a bit disingenuous, but except for the lover, there is little similarity between Aunt Lily of the memoirs and Albertine. (There may be more of grandmother Sophie Newhouse in Albertine, and something of Hellman's mother in Lily—a rich girl who was afraid of her mother and married to a poor man.)

Probably the most puzzling and incredible of the characters in *Toys* is Lily—but there she is in *An Unfinished Woman*, as twelve-year-old "Lillian." The panic-stricken jealousy—the fear of losing love; the ambivalence toward money and its power; the simplistic, fanatical allegiance to what she called "truth"—all were stages in Hellman's own adolescence. She, too, became incoherent under stress, and prone to self-injury. While the incident of the seance and the "knife of truth" in the play does not appear in the memoirs, it is typical of the kind of adventure young Lillian had in her pursuit of truth in New Orleans.

Toys in the Attic is both troubling and fascinating to read, and was a great success on the stage. As literature, however, it seems to need the memoirs too much—it is too incomplete and elliptical on its own. Characters that are mysterious or improbable in the context of the play become clear and credible only in the memoirs. And of course, contemporary critics lacked this tool for reference. Their judgments of the play were often contradictory— what one critic liked, another deplored. Some thought the first two acts were overplotted, others thought they dragged, and nothing happened until act three. But on

the whole the critics welcomed the professionalism of a
Hellman play, and considered *Toys in the Attic* to be
one of her best. So, also, did the audiences; the play ran
for 556 performances, second only in popularity to *The
Children's Hour*. It won the Drama Critics Circle Award
for the best American play of the season.

In looking back at Hellman's work as a playwright,
it is tempting to try to reduce all her plots and characters
to repeated formulas and types. Such an exercise can be
performed, of course, on any writer's body of work, but
the demands of the stage and of her favorite genre, the
realistic well-made melodrama, make Hellman's plays particularly vulnerable to this kind of analysis. I have already
pointed to some similarities in structure and characterization in the plays, but more interesting is the moral
point of view that unifies both the plays and the memoirs.
This is her concept of both active and passive evil, the
sins produced by both commission and omission.

Herman Melville, whose work Hellman had read
and taught, must have seemed a kindred soul to her in
his portrayal of evil in *Moby Dick*. Like Melville, Hellman watches evil fulfill itself not only through the de-
moniac—through the mad avenging Ahab—but also
through the "mere unaided virtue" of the first mate,
Starbuck, and the good-humored ignorance and medioc-
rity of the Stubbs and Flasks of this world.

The characters who endure in Hellman's world, are
those who live their lives according to inner rules of
decent behavior—of not making trouble for other people
and of facing the truth when others are deluded. They
are an often helpless minority, but they tacitly affirm the
existence of goodness in the face of evil. In *Moby Dick*
the lone survivor is the outcast, Ishmael. But he owed his
life and that "survival," with all its connotations, to his
friendship with the noble savage, Queequeg. The equiv-
alent of Queequeg in Hellman's work are the blacks, the

servants who are really the masters and mistresses because they can withstand hardship, and because they see the truth under appearances.

These characters began with Agatha in *The Children's Hour*, appeared in some form in *every* play, ending with probably the most minor character of them all, Gus, the black iceman in *Toys in the Attic*. When he advises the sisters to get themselves a nice cat, now that Julian is gone, he has spoken more truth and wisdom than ever entered the heads of the other characters. This kind of earthy insight was to be the touchstone of value in the memoirs, where it came to Hellman through two black women, Sophronia and Helen.

III

The Memoirs

5

○○○○○○○○○○○○○○○ ○○○○○○○○○○○○○○○○○○○○○○○ ○○○○○○○○○○○○○○○

Form and Theme—
"Through This Time
and That Time . . ."

Hellman's interest in the theater and playwriting waned in the early 1960s. She had begun to establish herself as a teacher of creative writing and literature and to explore the materials and forms that would shape the memoirs. The process had already begun, of course, when she dipped into those materials for *Toys in the Attic*, her last original play (to date).

As each volume of the memoirs appeared, it was heralded by previews—excerpts published as articles— and by much promotional fanfare. New work by Hellman was front-page material for the Sunday *New York Times Book Review* and major journals and newspapers throughout the country. All three volumes became bestsellers, commanding the attention (if not always the approval) of the critical as well as the popular readership. *An Unfinished Woman* (1969) won the National Book Award in the category of Arts and Letters. *Pentimento* (1973) became a Book-of-the-Month Club selection, and *Scoundrel Time*, after twenty-three weeks on the best-seller list, set off a controversy that lingered for months in newspapers and literary journals. Hellman's achievement brought her a multiplicity of new awards and honorary degrees. Scheduled to appear soon was the film based on "Julia," a chapter in *Pentimento*; Hellman had been offered over a half million dollars for the film rights to the series.[1]

Most readers responded to the books not as great literature, which reviewers sometimes made them out to be, but as a group of entertaining stories, some about well-known people and past events, but most of them about a person—or "persona"—named Lillian: a neurotic, rebellious character who stumbled from turned ankle to turned ankle in the general direction of heroism. But Hellman's memoirs have a deeper dimension, and so, of course, do the portraits of herself and others.

An Unfinished Woman is subtitled "a memoir" and *Pentimento* "a book of portraits." But the differences in mechanical structure are more apparent than real. The first book is built as a narrative, not strictly chronological, but still chiefly linear in movement from past to present and back again, relating events and persons to time and to each other. The second, *Pentimento*, is constructed as a series of portraits, each a unit, including group portraits and landscapes. But *An Unfinished Woman* also contains portraits—the last three chapters are the essays on Dorothy Parker, Helen (Hellman's cook and friend), and Dashiell Hammett. And the portraits in *Pentimento* are strung together in a loose chronological sequence, over the same time span as *An Unfinished Woman*.

Differences in the forms of the separate chapters or portraits are also deceptive. At first glance they seem to fall into three categories: the cluster of anecdotes or brief reminiscences grouped around a period or a subject; the diaries; and the dramatic tales—short stories told dramatically, like plays or film scripts. But a closer look reveals that the anecdotes may be clustered to illustrate a theme, and a diary may turn out to be a mysterious quest or a dramatic tale.

More interesting than the way Hellman organizes her materials is the way she sees them. The books are memoirs, rather than autobiographies, because their concentration seems, at least, to be upon the ambience of the writer rather than upon the writer herself. True, they reveal the author, but in carefully selected times, places, and company. Even in the anecdotes and diaries she is both narrator and protagonist, in a series of short, self-contained dramas.

As speaker and actress, Hellman is the principal unifier of the memoirs, but recurrent settings and characters also help to unify the books as they did her life. The bayou and the city of New Orleans, the sea near Cape Cod, the farm in Pleasantville, New York—any or all of these may surface to memory as she records an event that takes place in New York City or Hollywood or Moscow or Spain. Hellman's parents, her New Orleans aunts, her black nurse, Sophronia, and her cook, Helen, and always, of course, Dashiell Hammett, are somewhere in the background even when the immediate story is not theirs.

Hellman's professional life in the theater and in Hollywood is given relatively little attention in her memoirs. Most of the expected backstage gossip and theatrical name-dropping is confined to one chapter in *Pentimento* with some incidental references where they are relevant. For Hellman's books do not belong in the stream of theatrical memoirs that flows from Fanny Kemble to Tallulah Bankhead, any more than they do to the sensational confessions of Tennessee Williams. Her work is much more in the tradition of the autobiographical writings of such literary artists as Stendhal, in *The Life of Henry Brulard*, W. B. Yeats in his *Autobiography*, and Henry James in *A Small Boy and Others* and *Notes of a Son and Brother*.[2]

Central to these memoirs, as to Hellman's, is the concept of the writer as portrait painter, seeing himself and others in shifting lights, from varied angles. The act of remembering is inevitably selective, and the result, for whatever reason—unconscious suppression, perhaps—is often vague. But the purpose of a memoir for these artists is not total recall, or historical accuracy, but as Henry James put it, "to evoke the image and repaint the scene," although past and present may be confused (or fused) in the same scene, which James said, "glimmers out of a thin golden haze."[3]

The picture painted by the memoirist, then, is part memory, part imagination—often arousing speculation in both the writer and the reader as to which is which. Hellman's purpose was never to write historical biography; she said that she did not want to be the "book-keeper" of her life. Time and again she will preface her materials with such comment as, "I have no clear memories of those days, those years, not of myself where and when, not of other people. I know only that . . ." etc. This is not simply an excuse for inaccuracy: it implies also that what is worth remembering, will be, and that the self-portrait of the writer may be painted in what he chooses to remember.

But Stendhal and James were novelists, and Yeats a poet. Their memoirs are discursive, rambling philosophically between remembered events. They do not limit themselves to tight construction—to any line of "plot" or "character"—but let their wit and imagination roam freely over the past and present. Lillian Hellman, however, is a playwright: a maker of tightly constructed theater pieces, and the best of her memoirs are tales told by a playwright—with plot, character, and carefully paced suspense. Her biography provides a narrative line on which to hang the separate, loosely related episodes; and if some of these owe their mechanical structure to the well-made play and the film script, they owe their thematic, or symbolic structure (when it is there) to a combination of sources—including nineteenth-century American fiction, psychoanalysis, and Christianity.

Hellman's style has often been called elliptical, as indeed it is. She may withhold information at one time, to release it later for dramatic effect; or she may leave us with an unanswered question: "What could they have been talking about?" or a tentative suggestion of an answer. But more often, she leaves the reader with a sense of a mysterious undercurrent of meaning. Some critics have called her style "portentous" (suggesting that it is also pretentious) while others have called it "mysteriously exciting." When the mysterious undercurrent is successful, a "figure in the carpet" (as Henry James called it) gradually emerges. The reader finds that the meaning of events, the motivations of characters, the selection of a setting, all coalesce in a pattern that illuminates the whole.

But "mystery" in Hellman's work serves many purposes, from the subtle to the obvious. Her teaching of Herman Melville to college students must have taught her some of the uses of ambiguity: she seems to believe as Melville did, that ambiguity often presents a truer version of our perceptions than could clarity or sharp distinction. Melville, like other writers, often attempted to understand himself and his characters in the light of myth and ritual, and came up with pre-Freudian psycho-analytic insights, and pre-Jungian archetypal images. Hellman is influenced by her knowledge of the methods of literary symbolism and by her own predilection toward the religious mythic interpretations of experience, and not least, by her own experience of psychoanalysis, with strong religious associations.

The language of the memoirs is what Hellman would call "pretend cool." It is casual, slangy, objective, humor-ous, self-deprecatory. But these qualities are often decep-tive. Sometimes they are masked, restrained expressions of intense and often irrational angers, fears, conflicts. No one knew the destructive danger of these emotions better than Hellman. In the memoirs she often mentions her debt to Dr. Gregory Zilboorg, the psychoanalyst who helped her understand and live with this part of herself. It was to him that she dedicated *Another Part of the*

Forest. Some of the family ghosts that she laid to rest in that play and *The Little Foxes* rise again in the memoirs.

Zilboorg was a prolific and distinguished writer, whose *A History of Medical Psychology* (with George Henry) is still a definitive text. At one period in his life he had also been a drama critic, and had translated Andreyev's *He Who Gets Slapped*. But one of Zilboorg's major interests lay in exploring the relationship between psychoanalysis and religion. *Mind, Medicine, and Man* and the posthumously published *Psychoanalysis and Religion* are collections of his essays on the subject. In these he tried to reconcile the two disciplines. Psychoanalysis and religion, he said, were two different, equally necessary "systems" and by no means incompatible. They had been considered mutually exclusive—chiefly because of Freud's atheism (Freud had called religion an illusion) and the psychological determinism of many of his disciples. Zilboorg thought that Christian doctrine and ritual could be helpful both to the analyst and his patient. He himself had been born a Russian Jew, but became a devout Roman Catholic.

In 1964, when she was in Israel reporting on the Pope's visit to that country, Hellman was reminded of Zilboorg by a Dominican priest who knew Zilboorg's work. Her response to that memory and to the face of the priest echoes through all the memoirs:

The fervent words, the intense face, took me back a long way, to the time when I was seven or eight years old in New Orleans and wandered one Sunday morning into a church whose denomination I don't remember, and possibly never knew, and was so moved by the sermon I didn't understand that I ran from the church crying to be good and never sinful, and fell down the steps and went on home, screaming, to have my knee fixed, knowing, as a child often senses the future, that I would all my life be stirred and comforted and discomforted [sic] by people of strong belief, and that I had better take myself along on home whenever that happened.[4]

One lesson, reflected in the memoirs, that Hellman must have learned from Zilboorg was his often repeated idea that love was essential to both religion and psychoanalysis: "[Religion] sees in love the means for ultimate salvation; [psychoanalysis] the means for ultimate health." But wherever Hellman got her "religious streak," as her friend John Hersey called it[5]—from her mother or the black women in her life or Zilboorg—it runs through the memoirs from the first chapter of *An Unfinished Woman* to the last chapter of *Pentimento*, and surfaces again in *Scoundrel Time*.

Nevertheless, these memoirs, obviously, are not religious, symbolic, or psychoanalytic documents. Some of them are simply anecdotal, freely associated recollections; others are, as I have said, dramatic tales drawn from a life, but not attempting a full chronology of that life, nor exclusively dedicated to biographical revelation. Hellman asks us to read a book about someone named Lillian Hellman, but to keep the character in the book and the author of the book separate. The narrator of the memoirs is also a *persona* or mask for the author, not necessarily a literal replica. The unity imposed on the work by this continuing *persona* never becomes completely clear to the reader—Hellman tells the truth but tells it slant (as Emily Dickinson would say). She consciously creates a legend and is as jealous of her privacy as she is conscious of the legend.

It is beyond the scope of this book—and the ability and intention of its author—to attempt a psychoanalysis of Lillian Hellman. Such presumptuousness always results in what Hellman called "Woolworth Freud." She has told us a great deal about herself in the memoirs, and I leave it to the reader to go beyond what is written there to find the "real" Lillian Hellman. She, herself, might say to the reader—with justice—"That is none of your business!"

The persona, the legend, is the same in all the books,

but each book is unique and deserves its own analysis. The most important difference between the two long books is in their thematic emphasis. *An Unfinished Woman* questions and explores the occasions and rites of initiation, the expiation of guilts, the meaning of suffering and survival—all of these in the context of a deepening insight into self. *Pentimento* seems to be thematically unified around the shapes of love: exploration takes the form of what Richard Poirier has called "emotional range-finding."[6] In the portrait chapters of *Pentimento*, Hellman ponders the nature of her deepest relationships to others. Of course, the two books combine or interchange themes at times: the last two chapters of *Pentimento* raise questions about suffering, guilt, and survival posed earlier in *An Unfinished Woman*. But this is an appropriate ending for the second book and brings the wheel full circle.

6

ooooooooooooooooooooooooooooooooooooooo oooooooooooooo

An Unfinished Woman

When asked about the writing of *An Unfinished Woman*, Hellman said,

It was *faute de mieux*, that book. I decided I didn't want to write for the theater, so what was I to do? I didn't want to do an autobiography—that would have been too pretentious for me. I had a lot of magazine pieces I'd done that hadn't been reprinted and I started to rewrite them. But I didn't like them. I thought, maybe now I can do better with the same memories.[1]

And she did. Some of the sections originating in magazine articles will be indicated below, but what Hellman selects from them has usually been transformed.

The organization of *An Unfinished Woman*, from chapter one through thirteen, is chronological. The last three chapters are portraits. The chronological chapters are arranged in pairs: each pair consists of a short introductory essay, followed by the actual story to be told. (In *Pentimento* Hellman avoids splitting the portraits into numbered chapters, but each one still opens with an introductory "exposition.") Hellman's childhood in New Orleans provides the material for chapters one-two; three-four take us through her early days in New York and her first job there; five-six cover her brief marriage, Hollywood, and first acquaintance with Dorothy Parker, Hemingway, Dashiell Hammett; seven-eight take her to Europe, and Spain during the revolution (1937). (Chap-

ter seven of *An Unfinished Woman* is further developed
as the "Julia" episode in *Pentimento*.) Chapter nine is
transitional, leading from the Spanish experience through
her own "turning toward radicalism." Chapters ten-eleven
cover her adventures in Russia in 1944-45; and twelve-
thirteen take her back to Russia in 1966-67. Chapters
fourteen, fifteen, and sixteen are the portraits of Dorothy
Parker, Helen (Hellman's friend and cook-housekeeper),
and Dashiell Hammett.

The chronological sections (1-13) fall into three
general periods: the southern childhood and adolescence;
young womanhood in New York and Hollywood—finding
herself emotionally and vocationally—and the European
adventures in Spain and Russia, spanning both past and
present—1937-1967. The sequence of these chapters is
obviously from youth to age; from the exploration of
beginnings and initiations to the later questioning of the
meanings of survival. But each initiation is a test, and
the passing of that test—no matter how early or how
tentative—is itself a "survival."

Typically, in the paired chapters of the memoirs, the
first provides background and speculation about the
meaning of a given period in Hellman's life: then the
"test" or event follows in the longer chapter. Chapter one
of *An Unfinished Woman* is a straightforward account of
her feelings toward her parents and others in the family,
including insights into her childhood, acquired much
later, after psychoanalysis. The actual escapades that made
for initiation and survival take place in chapter two.

Hellman always loved her father's family, especially
the two New Orleans aunts, Hannah and Jenny. Her
father was lively and charming, as were his sisters. Her
mother was quietly withdrawn, eccentric, hurt in many
ways by a dominating mother and a philandering husband, and deeply frightened by the "dangerously botched"
birth of her only child. She turned for solace to religion

—not caring which sect, just happy in a church. The mother's passivity and strange fears were irritating to the daughter, who was to spend a lifetime expiating her childhood guilt for that irritability, and for transferring love due her mother to the black wet-nurse, Sophronia, "the first and most certain love of my life."

Hellman's attitude toward her mother's wealthy family was complicated. On one hand she hated their money-based values, and their ill-gotten gains at the expense of the southern poor, black and white. But this was compounded with self-hatred when she saw in herself some of those same values and a need for the symbols of wealth and the life style it can buy. We have already seen the difficulties this family involvement made for Hellman in the writing of *The Little Foxes*. In *An Unfinished Woman* she says that "after *The Little Foxes* was written and put away, this conflict was to grow less important, as indeed the picture of my mother's family was to grow dim and fade away." The ghost of the wronged mother was temporarily laid to rest, as we have seen, in the characters of Birdie in *The Little Foxes* and Lavinia in *Another Part of the Forest*. But the same dybbuk is invoked and exorcised again in *An Unfinished Woman* in the sketch of the long-suffering, gentle mother, and Hellman's final statement, "My mother was dead for five years before I knew I loved her very much." That knowledge would have come in 1940, about the time that Hellman began her analysis with Zilboorg.

Hellman's childhood, she tells us, was torn by other conflicts and other guilts, many of which had to do with being an only child, demanding total love, and being insecure at the impossibility of having it; using her power over her parents to punish them, and ultimately herself. The most severe conscious life-long conflict, dominating her edgy relationships with others, took the form, even in childhood she says, of "the stubborn, relentless, driving desire to be alone as it came into conflict with the desire

not to be alone when I wanted not to be." She realized
early that for what she calls a "nature" like hers the way
would not be easy. This self-knowledge came when, as a
child, she made for herself a retreat in the great fig tree
on the grounds of her aunt's boarding house in New
Orleans. The narrative—or drama—begins in chapter
two, with a description of Lillian in the tree.

On her annual six-month visit to New Orleans, from
the time she was about eight until she was sixteen, Lillian
would often skip school, climb the fig tree with her lunch
and books and fishing pole, and spend the day there reading and spying on the passers-by below. Her flossy school
dress and patent leather slippers hung on a twig to keep
them neat until her return to civilization. Many American
readers—women as well as men—have done something
like this as a child, with the same ritualization of privacy
and growth, even to the excitement of fishing in a muddy
gutter for whatever life might be there. Some archetypal
form of this experience appears throughout literature in
memoirs and fiction. For Hellman it marked the beginning of a lifelong need for balance between the crowds
and company of the city and the solitary one-to-one relationship of a human being with the natural world. The
little feminine Huck Finn in the tree foreshadows the
woman who lived with Dashiell Hammett on a farm with
a pond in Pleasantville, New York; and later, the woman
who divided her year between New York City and an
island off Cape Cod. The fig-tree sequence in *An Unfinished Woman* is not completely serious in tone; it has
its funny aspects.

The next New Orleans episode begins also as comedy: after a puppy-love affair and some experience with
adult pecadilloes—namely, her father's—the fourteen-
year-old Lillian runs away from home. But what follows
is a tale of terror, narrated in the detached voice of a
bemused adult. The young girl takes a nightmare journey

through adolescence toward a religious and sexual initiation. She must find her way not only through the city but through hurts and jealousies and attachments that she does not understand.

The episode begins when Lillian's father scolds her angrily, in front of her aunts' boarders. Her first reaction to the scolding is prophetic: "My mother left the room when my father grew angry with me. . . . I sat on the couch, astonished at the pain in my head. I tried to get up from the couch, but one ankle turned and I sat down again, knowing for the first time the rampage that could be caused in me by anger." Lillian's mother tries to comfort her, but a piece of angel cake is no palliative for the imagined loss of a father's love. Lillian tramps off down St. Charles Avenue—a runaway with a few dollars in a little red purse. Her first adventure comes when she passes a mansion with a smaller version of itself—a doll's house—on its back lawn. A policeman approaches, and to escape him she hides in the doll's house. There she curls up among the miniatures of ornate furniture—a big little girl, like Alice down the rabbit hole.

From the symbolic doll's house, a step forward perhaps, from the womb, the young Lillian finds her next hiding place in a church—the St. Louis Cathedral. There she composed the prayer which she says was to become an obsession during the next five years: "God forgive me, Papa forgive me, Mama forgive me, Sophronia, Jenny, Hannah and all others, through this time and that time, in life and in death."

And from the church her flight takes her to the red-light district. Here she is frightened by some terrifying versions of adult sexuality—whores who shout at her and an old "flasher" who exposes himself. She buys food, and falls asleep with it behind some bushes, only to wake in hysteria when she sees two hungry rats staring at her. She runs back to the church, pounds on the door scream-

ing, but no one comes. The night ends in the ladies' room
at the railroad station. Lillian is suffering her first men-
strual cramps. She throws away her soiled underwear,
and her face in the mirror tells her, with a certain adolescent bathos, "I had gotten older."

She is finally rescued, as she was always to be sym-
bolically rescued, by her surrogate mother, Sophronia.
By mentioning Sophronia's name, Lillian has been taken
in for the night in a boarding house in the black district.
There she sleeps soundly, and wakes to find Sophronia
and her father at her bedside. Her father finally apolo-
gizes for the scolding, but makes her feel guilty when he
adds, "You should not have made me say it." And this
evokes her penitential prayer, "God forgive me, Papa
forgive me, Mama forgive me, Sophronia, Jenny. . . ."
When her father hears what she is saying, he asks—and
it's a significant question—"Where do we start your
training as the first Jewish nun on Prytania Street?" It
has already started, of course.

Lillian tells her father at the end of this chapter
that she is "changing life." She has experienced not only
intimations of adulthood but also a new insight into the
power and the problems of an only child. And equally
important, the escapade gave Hellman a "useful and dangerous" lifelong theory of survival: "If you are willing
to take the punishment, you are halfway through the
battle. That the issue may be trivial, the battle ugly, is
another point."

If this were fiction, the symbolic pattern might make
the tale too pat, too allegorical. Lillian is almost a female
counterpart of Nathaniel Hawthorne's Robin, the young
initiate in "My Kinsman, Major Molineux." But we cannot quarrel with Hellman's memory—or dreams—and
certainly not with her craftsmanship. It is a great yarn,
wittily told, with much more charm than this outline of
the "pattern" would suggest. Indeed, it is not until we

reach the Russian diaries, the chronicle of another journey a half century later, that we find again such symbolic literary structure.

The rebelliousness against authority that led the child Lillian through the streets of New Orleans, grew more intense in her late teens and is with her still—still making trouble for herself and other people, in spite of Sophronia's advice, "Don't go through life making trouble for people," and Hellman's own efforts to control it. Some of her anger was channeled into the plays, where it is often given a moral or political base. That moral indignation is also in the memoirs, but in *An Unfinished Woman* and *Pentimento*, Hellman faces the fact that moral indignation may at times be only a mask for personal pique, for irritability at an insult or an invasion of privacy. Often—not always—the old prayer for forgiveness is implied, even as she smashes a chair or slaps a face.

The saving grace from either diatribe or sentimentality is the wry, often rueful humor with which Hellman looks at herself. This is the tone of the chapters that take us through her first job, her brief marriage, the Hollywood experience, and the trips to Europe in the 1930s. We learn very little here or in *Pentimento* about her intellectual development as a writer; but her vocational progress in that direction began with her job in publishing.

Life at Horace Liveright's was notable chiefly, as I have said, for the variety of its parties, which contributed to Hellman's social and sexual education. (Her encounters with authors and manuscripts were interesting but incidental.) It is in the context of the Liveright situation that she uses the term "pretend cool" to describe the attitude of her generation toward sex. She had no patience with the prurient curiosity of some of the older "flaming youth" about her own generation, nor with the weepy romantic sentimentality of some of the "lady writers."

But her own cool was all pretend. At nineteen, just before taking the Liveright job, she had had a brief "affair" (the quotation marks are hers) with a young man who seemed to be using her to make his best friend jealous. "The few months it lasted," she says, "did not mean much to me, but I have often asked myself whether I underestimated the damage that so loveless an arrangement made on [sic] my future."

Some of the anecdotes about life at Liveright's are hilarious, but underneath it all is the serious fact that she became pregnant and went through a stoic, lonely abortion (to the admiration of her colleagues). A half year later she married the man involved, Arthur Kober. Neither an affair nor marriage, nor romantic love was ever to be a happy experience for her. The long association with Hammett had some bad times; it was an indispensable fact of her life for thirty-one years, but hardly "happy" or passionately "romantic." There were connotations in her father's joking reference to the "Jewish nun on Prytania Street" that would be echoed later in references to Hellman—by Hellman and others—as a "Puritan" or "Calvinist." The terms applied not only to her "religious streak" but also to a shyness or uneasiness about sex, her protestations to the contrary notwithstanding.[2] But Hellman's inhibitions were more of a nuisance to her than an obsession: she had too many other fish to fry. Romantic love could be—as it was in the plays—a silly, potentially destructive force, best ignored.

Hellman remembered the years of her marriage and her introduction to Hollywood as foggy, tedious, uncertain. It was not until she met Hammett, was divorced, and began to write in earnest that her life took a real direction. The chapters (5-6) in *An Unfinished Woman* on this period begin with Hollywood, then flash forward and backward in time, wherever associations lead. The 1929 visit to Germany receives only slight mention. References to later European trips serve, here, only to pinpoint her meetings with the temperamental, flamboyant older generation of writers who clustered around Gerald and Sara Murphy, their hosts and patrons.

Hellman treats us to some fine gossipy anecdotes about feuds between Hemingway and Fitzgerald, Hammett and Hemingway, Dorothy Parker and Hemingway, Dorothy Parker and Hammett. But she never felt a part of this group; they were too ego-involved, too hypocritical.

It was witty, all of it, but I remember feeling awkward: my generation was perhaps all round duller and certainly less talented, but loyalty, or the rhetoric of it, had come back into fashion with the depression, and these . . . remarkable people . . . came from another world and time.

Some of the most important events of Hellman's personal "world and time" at this period are postponed until *Pentimento*—especially her beginning success as a playwright and the story of "Julia." In *An Unfinished Woman*, the European trips of 1934 to 1944 and after, are concerned with Hellman's growth in relationship to events in Spain and Russia. She writes as a sympathetic outsider in Spain in 1937, and in Russia in 1944-1945. But on her return to Russia in 1967, the world that interests her most is her own; the "nature" of the aging visitor, not the country visited. Her initiations; her survivals— what have they meant?

The Spanish adventure takes the form of a diary; daily entries made in 1937 are remembered, parenthetically, in 1968, but the action of the narrative takes place in 1937. Upon her arrival in Spain, Hellman was briefed on the political intricacies of the revolution, told the progress of the war so far, the atrocities, the numbers of casualties, but this is not, she says, how she learns things, and not the way she tells them to us. Her learning took place in encounters with human beings as they endured the bombings, the hunger, and all the losses of war.

But in spite of many vivid, stirring moments, the essay is marred by suggestions of mystery that never take shape into a pattern. In the intricate design of this "carpet," there is no underlying "figure," or I haven't seen it. Hellman remembers the human dramas, but she tries too consciously to use the techniques of theatrical drama to present them to the reader. She will introduce a character or a group in one diary entry, pose a question about them, and leave the reader cliff-hanging for the answer until a later entry. Sometimes there is no answer: a mystery or premonition may be suggested when characters are introduced but may never be resolved or defined.

Of course, some of the memorable portraits are not mysterious: the hungry people—peasants, city people, guests in expensive hotels—all famished. In Hellman's experience, they are willing to share what they have and grateful for the few things others would share with them. She met engaged, dedicated writers such as Gustav Regler, Otto Simon, and, of course, Hemingway with his apparent enjoyment of the "fireworks"—the bombing of Madrid—and his reluctant macho approval of Hellman when she braved the bombardment in order to make a radio broadcast.

But the reader remains taunted by the fuzzy, ominous characterizations. Who—or what—is that strange couple —the man in black and his companion, the "nun *fanée*?" (Hellman meets them at intervals in Valencia; then seeks them out before she leaves.) What is all that talk with this couple about religion, leading up to a final sexual shocker? Are these Jamesian decadent—if not incestuous —Europeans, near relatives of Teck (himself partly out of James) in *Watch on the Rhine*? Or—oh, no—are they a parable of Franco and the Church? And what about the young Frenchman named Pascal whose sickness and death conclude the chapter? Who *is* the father that he will not see—the waiter? And does he refuse the last rites because, in his delirium, he thinks he is in Spain and the church there is corrupt?

Maybe the 1938 diaries were just too far away for Hellman herself to remember what they "meant." The overtones of mystery and the techniques of melodrama cannot keep them from looking like literary patchwork. The patches are pasted, however, against a background of the pervasive themes of initiation and survival. The Spanish war enforced Hellman's knowledge of the reality and the imminence of death. She carried with her still in 1968, a *memento mori* in the form of some ornaments taken from the wreckage of a bombed-out Spanish home. And then, from Pascal and from the young wounded soldiers in the International Brigade, she learned—and was to relearn from her friend "Julia" and from Hammett—that imprisonment, suffering, death itself are not too much for some people to pay in the service of an ideal. And that such a martyrdom has always been, in mystical or religious terms, its own "survival" or implicit resurrection.

Hellman is groping toward this knowledge in the Spanish interlude just as she is groping her way toward her own kind of radicalism. She knew that she had become seriously politicized late. Hammett had influenced her, of course, but one source of the tension between them was her inability to align herself with any specific revolutionary cause. "Rebels," she explains, "seldom make good revolutionaries, perhaps because organized action, even union with other people, is not possible for them."

The trip to Russia in 1944 was apparently not the product of radical political convictions. Hellman had just collaborated on the rather innocuously pro-Russian film, *North Star*; two of her plays were in rehearsal in Moscow, and both Washington and Ambassador Litvinov thought that she would make a good cultural emissary. Her official, but strictly civilian status was to give her entry into high diplomatic circles as well as to the fighting front.

The prelude to the Russian diary is a vivid, sometimes funny, chronicle of the harrowing two-week flight to Moscow. Hellman was the only passenger on the Russian two-engine plane that took off from Alaska to fly across Siberia. She was treated as the guest of honor—as far as that was possible—and her "escort" and translator was a nineteen-year-old Russian boy who spoke almost no English and called her "Miss Hell." The plane was unheated, the trip bitterly cold, and Hellman arrived in Moscow with not only her usual sprained ankle, but a bad case of pneumonia—among other ailments. The wartime deprivation and suffering of the Russians, however, impressed her more than her own, and this chapter (9) ends on a familiar note: Hellman sees the greatness of the human spirit in what it is capable of surviving. A young Russian soldier who had been shot in the face tried to smile at her through his mutilation—"It was in the next few hours that I felt a kind of exaltation I had never felt before."

The Russian chapters do not lean entirely on the diary form as did the Spanish chapters, although some paragraphs do have dateline headings. Hellman never stays very long with the actual time period of the diary, but slides forward into the present as she writes, often comparing what she remembers now to what the diaries recorded then. 1944-1945 is remembered in 1966-1967 (chapters 12-13), but both are seen in retrospect from 1968. The unifying movement is between retrospection and introspection, and as the narrative proceeds, introspection becomes the dominant mode. The years of 1944-1945 are seen in retrospect; those from 1966 move in-

creasingly inward; their subject is less the past than it is
the present, less the outward event than the inner life
of the memoirist.

The visit to Russia in 1944-1945 had been described
by Miss Hellman in an article in *Collier's* magazine, "I
Meet the Front Line Russians" (March 1945). That
contemporary report and this one in *An Unfinished
Woman* are almost (with the exception of a few passages)
entirely different. The *Collier's* article begins with a glum
description of the five-day journey to the front, but then
turns into a cheerful narrative about two girls (Hellman
and her translator) on a great lark to the Russian lines.
They are entertained by the gallant soldiers, who are sick
of fighting and cheered by the presence and the admiration of the two young ladies. The article was slanted for
the slick magazine in which it appeared, and presented
a friendly, optimistic view of our wartime Russian ally.[3]

The friendship with Russia is still there, in *An Unfinished Woman*, but the picture has changed drastically.
Hellman stayed at the ambassador's mansion, but spent
much of her time those first weeks in Moscow at the
Hotel Metropole, "a grubby joint, but lively" and inhab-
ited mostly by foreign journalists and businessmen. The
escapades of the hotel's inhabitants make up a series of
"comedy dramas," as Hellman calls them, whose very
triviality provides relief from the hungry winter outside.

The tone of the visit to the front is now somber. The
cheerful girl is preoccupied by her fear of the journey,
which finally yields to a kind of resignation when she is
on the train and "in other hands." The Russians are
kind; they appear as characters in a drama, with clearly
differentiated personalities. But over them all—Hellman
and the soldiers—hangs the specter of the German occu-
pation, brought home to her by the dreadful remains at
the ovens in the concentration camp at Maidenek. This
horror diminishes all other fears. Hellman joins the Russians in their anger and disgust at the Nazi deserters—

former Storm Troopers—who tried to grovel or lie their
way into Russian protection. This later version of the
1944 journey is more angrily anti-Nazi than it is cheer-
fully pro-Russian.

The chapters on the return to Russia in 1966 and
again in 1967 incorporate reminiscences of previous
years. Events in Russia in 1966 take Hellman back to
events of 1944; and these, in turn, lead forward to memories of life on the farm at Pleasantville, of Hammett,
and of the House Un-American Activities Committee
hearings in 1952, that brought the loss of the farm and
a change of fortune for her and for him. These times and
memories seem to be freely associated, but they have an
agonizing impact upon Hellman. The images, again, form
variations on the theme of survival—on what it means
to have lived through pain and punishment and loss. To
face these remembrances with self-insight is to raise the
inevitable questions of one's responsibility for the past,
whether guilt or credit. And to look at that past in the
context of a long lifetime, one continuum in which past,
present, and future make a whole, is to face also the
future—to face age and change. This is what happens in
these last two chapters of the memoir as narrative, before
Hellman leaves it for the portrait form.

She remembers that as the plane landed in Moscow,
in 1966, she found herself crying, and wondering why.
"What fragment at the bottom of the pot was the kettle-
spoon scraping that it had not reached before?" She
knows that the first level of disturbance is the knowledge
that she is aging; that the woman who made the plane
trip across Siberia in 1944 would never have the strength
to do that again. But this kind of self-pity is not in character for her, and she laughs herself out of it, momen-
tarily at least, when she hears the unidiomatic English of
the Russian stewardess's announcement of the landing:
". . . . We have come to the end of the road and we must
take our parting. . . ." Hellman suggests to the stewardess

that she find a less mournful sentence. But the stewardess resents the correction, and her angry face becomes to Hellman the face of a big bullying girl in New Orleans who used to hit her when she was six. Hellman rejects that image with, "I said to myself, to hell with this memory nonsense," and goes forward to meet Raya, her old friend and interpreter of twenty-two years before.

But this memory nonsense will not go to hell—will not be suppressed—just at a word. The threatening face of the stewardess introduces a long series of images of injury, loss, and survival, all finally summarized in the ironic truth of the landing speech, "we must now take our parting," however that may be interpreted. The images flow through Hellman's dreams, waking her at night, disturbing and crippling her daytime life. They occur in her meetings with others—Raya, Tanya, Captain K: long-time Russian friends who have also suffered losses, imprisonment, or mutilation—real and metaphorical— and have witnessed the same and death, for friends and lovers.

Is it Hellman the memoirist or Hellman the novelist manqué who in a gloomy hotel in Moscow finds herself digging up her own "frozen roots"? And who, on that same boozy sleepless night, knocks over a large china figure of a Greek athlete and crawls around the floor trying to find his broken hand? Only to dream then of hers and Hammett's injuries and losses; and to remember the injury she may have done—but had to do—to her father. One incident takes her back twenty years to a memory of Gregory Zilboorg's telling her that her father was senile and must be hospitalized. "He [her father] blamed me for his being in the hospital and thus I lost my father, as he lost his mind, for two years before his death."

The theme of the strong man—father, husband, lover, friend—brought low by injury or age or weakness is reflected in Hellman's own psychic wounds and moves throughout this chapter to the end. Her good friend, Captain K, the Russian soldier whom she had met in 1945 when he was "just out of the hospital after a bad leg wound," greets her in Moscow in 1966. His leg wound was serious, but worse for him was the loss, during combat, of the thesis on American literature that had been his lifelong interest. Hellman tries to help by discussing American writers with him and promising to send him books. Their talk lingers on male novelists—Hemingway, Faulkner, Mailer. One wonders at the coincidence that all three writers were intrigued with the theme of mutilated or impotent strength. And Hellman and the captain also discuss the great film director, Serge Eisenstein, whom Hellman called "one of the most forceful and brilliant men I have ever met"—and whom she still admired after she learned of his weaknesses.

When Hellman meets Captain K again in 1967, they are like two old wounded soldiers. This time they talk about her and the problems she does not really want to talk about—her aging, her sense of mistakes and loss. The captain asks about Zilboorg, and Hellman replies vaguely that she supposed the psychoanalysis helped. Her old cantakerousness is still there, even when she tells him the truth: "I don't like the theater any more and yet it is what I do best. I have cut myself away from it, don't go much, don't learn, don't even want to. And I am getting old and I can't understand how that happened to me."

The last entry in the 1967 diary recounts a visit to the hospital bed of the Russian poet, Olga Bergholz. Hellman is uneasy and irritated until she discovers that she has been reminded of another writer, Dorothy Parker, also lying ill at the time in America. And she goes back to the hotel to write Dottie a letter to cheer her up—she was to die six weeks later. The comic letter that Hellman wrote that night in Moscow was found among Dorothy Parker's few papers and is printed in full in her portrait, the first of three to conclude *An Unfinished Woman*.

"Dorothy Parker"

Like Parker's own work, the portrait is a mixture of wit and pathos. The friendship of Dottie and "Lilly" spanned a period of thirty-six years. It began with dislike, but ripened into understanding and acceptance, on both sides, of each other's quirks—of which there were many. They never agreed on some subjects, especially men, but they were nourished by each other's company and enjoyed each other's sense of humor.

In a newspaper interview, Hellman said that she could never have done that portrait if Parker had been living. "She'd have been pained. We had an elaborately polite relationship—I don't think we said an unpleasant thing in all the years."[4] Parker is usually remembered as the author of sophisticated, polished, and quotable verse, and, as a person, for her gaiety, her mischievous humor, and sharp repartee.

Hellman does nothing to damage that image in the portrait, but there were other truths about Parker, and Hellman presents them with tact and affection. Saddest was the self-destructive quality of some of Parker's clowning: Hellman says she "wanted the put-down from everybody." Then there was her drinking, some early suicide attempts, and chronic disorganization. Toward the end, Parker misplaced—or hid from herself—some large uncashed checks and was convinced that she was poor. But even this delusion comes off as a sort of gallantry in Hellman's eulogy: "She never had much, but what she had she didn't care about, and that was very hat-over-the-windmill stuff in a sick lady of seventy-four."

Parker is a character in the *dramatis personae* of *An Unfinished Woman*, and the image we have seen of her before this, in early chapters, may be more light-hearted, but it is not inconsistent with the final one. In the last years, when Parker was writing little and drinking much, Hellman found her company depressing, saw

less of her, then blamed herself for neglecting a brave,
still wisecracking invalid. But Parker never doubted
Lilly's friendship, and made her the executor of her
small estate. Hellman's tribute captures the contradictions
in Parker's personality: her need for both success and
failure, for love and rejection, admiration and scorn.
Dorothy Parker summed up her own character in the
much-quoted lines:

> Three be the things I shall have till I die:
> Laughter and hope and a sock in the eye.

"Helen"

Helen Jackson, Miss Hellman's friend and cook for
twenty-odd years, is the subject of the penultimate portrait. If it had been placed last—as the "ultimate" portrait
—"Helen" would have closed the circle from Hellman's
New Orleans childhood to the present—1969, the time
of writing the memoir. For this chapter concerns not only
Helen, now dead for three months, but Sophronia, who
had died thirty years before. As the images of the two
women merge in the writer's mind, the time-gap between
them closes.

In actuality, the two black women were individual
personalities, but as symbols of a cultural phenomenon
of the American south, and of forces in Hellman's life,
they flow together in this dreamlike narrative. Only an
American southerner close to Hellman's age could understand the subtle intermingling of love and hate between and among southern blacks and whites, especially
in this stormy period of integration and black liberation.

The essay is a form of the dramatic tale, constructed
in scenes like a film script. It begins with a dreamlike
reverie, leading to a dream sequence in which the characters of Helen and Sophronia blend, then separate, as
first one, then the other, dominates the action. There is

a long flashback to Hellman's childhood, with Sophronia
as the setter of standards, but the protagonist throughout
the film script is really Helen, that "far-out Christian
lady." Her generosity, her refusal to hate—or to acknowl-
edge that she does—constitutes her own kind of pride
and activism. This truth about Helen's character comes
home only slowly to Hellman, the antagonist in the drama.

The process of discovery starts where it often does
for Hellman, in recollection of her love of the sea and
her childlike pleasure in the life of ponds and streams
and the shore's edge, whether in New Orleans or a half
century later at Martha's Vineyard. One need not know
the Freudian or Jungian interpretations of water imagery
to watch Hellman always linking it with initiation, survival, and insight—birth, death, and symbolic rebirth. In
the beautiful opening reverie she acknowledges that digging about on the shore is like digging in one's unconscious, in dreams, for what might lie there, to find on
awakening "the answer to a long-forgotten problem."

One stormy night in Cambridge, Massachusetts, when
Hellman was teaching at Harvard, she was awakened by
the crash of a ceiling light to the floor. Still half asleep,
she stared at the shattered lamp on the floor and remembered poking about on the beach and finding a mangled
watch there. (A Daliesque image if ever there was one.)
It had belonged to Helen, who had concealed from Hellman the fact that Hellman's dog had brought the watch
to the beach. "She didn't want to tell me that my dog,
who loved her but didn't love me, could have done anything for which he could be blamed." The meaning of the
recollection is suddenly clear: "Of course . . . they were
one person to you, these two black women you loved more
than you ever loved any other women: Sophronia from
childhood, Helen so many years later. . . ."

Hellman sees a difference in her relationship to the
two, however. Sophronia was always the protector, the
tolerant loving mother and strict judgmental father in one.

Helen was the loyal generous friend and equal, whose combination of love and judgment often angered Hellman. There was guilt toward Sophronia—Hellman had not gone to her funeral. But then she had not known when Sophronia died, and her sin of omission was inadvertent—but to Hellman guilt is always too complicated to be expiated by simple cause-and-effect reasoning. Sophronia would have expected her at the funeral and she should have been there. But the guilt to be expiated in the present narrative is that arising from her anger toward Helen. It also involves inadvertent "omission," a failure of insight, like that of the narrator in some of Henry James's fiction, who fails to comprehend the import of the behavior of others until too late. (Daisy Miller "would have appreciated one's esteem.")

There are complex reasons in the essay for the failure of insight and for misunderstanding on both sides. A liberal white is impatient with a conservative black, whose values are Christian and human rather than racial or political. As an angry white liberal, it is hard for Hellman to accept Helen's loyalty to some white people, even to herself. Helen claims that (as a good Christian) she has never hated. But Hellman tries to convince her that this is not true; she has hated, and in a way hates Hellman, her white employer. To her dismay, Hellman succeeds in arousing Helen's anger and rebellion—but not overtly against white people: only against the "slavery" of working for a demanding, unpredictable, erratic "northern" employer. Helen says she was a cook in the south; now she's a slave. Then it is Hellman's turn to rage. She calls Helen a liar, and stomps off to Katonah, New York, and Hammett. Then as usual, Hammett reminds her that she will be sorry for her anger: she realizes that there are some things it is too late for her and Helen to talk about, goes home, and they are reconciled.

In 1963, Hellman covered the freedom march of two

hundred thousand blacks on Washington under the leadership of Martin Luther King. Her report appeared in the *Ladies' Home Journal* under the title, "Sophronia's Grandson goes to Washington."[5] (Some of that material has been incorporated in this portrait of Helen, including a long flashback to childhood and Sophronia.) But Sophronia's grandson, Orin, never showed up in Washington, and when, in *An Unfinished Woman*, he is finally brought to see Hellman in New York, he turns out to be a drug addict—what Helen calls "a no-good punkie-junkie." Helen does what she can to help Orin handle withdrawal, and then sends him on his way. He gives no sign of any intention to reform.

But Helen's anger is aimed not at the society that could destroy a young man—as it had her own daughter —but at the "big city" and the universal human weakness that has always yielded to temptation there. The young uprooted black from the rural south has been destroyed by the urban north—just like the country boy from New Hampshire in the melodrama *The Old Homestead*. The romantic pastoral is still alive and well in Helen's consciousness. To Hellman she says, "South got its points, no matter what you think. Even if just trees." And, of course, with her own need for "trees"—or the shore—Hellman must accept this, even if the sentiment plays havoc with her liberal politics.[6]

Helen befriended other young blacks whom Hellman had met in Washington and elsewhere. After Helen's death, one of the young men, George, comes to see Hellman and tells her of Helen's generosity to himself and others. This becomes the dramatic closing scene of a screenplay. Printed in that form, the script might look like this:

GEORGE: . . . Then she gave me one hundred dollars. Eighty-five for me, she said, or wherever I wanted to give it. Fifteen for Orin when I found him.

HELLMAN: *Orin? Orin?*

GEORGE: He's still hanging around. She always gave him a little money. But he ain't going to get this fifteen, 'cause I ain't going to find him. She was some far-out lady, Mrs. Jackson. Some far-out Christian lady.

HELLMAN: Sure was.

GEORGE: I hope you feel better. Next time I'm here, I'll come to see you. (exit)

HELLMAN: (to herself) But he never has come to see me again. (She looks off in the distance. Camera moves in tight on her haunted face. Ocean music from first scene up and over. Deep, slow pull–away shot of her figure as she bends down to pick up something on the beach. Fadeout).

"Dashiell Hammett"

The final essay, the portrait of Dashiell Hammett, had been written in 1965 as the introduction to *The Big Knockover*, a collection of Hammett's short stories. Before that, it had been published in *The New York Review of Books*. Hammett, as a presence, is well known to the reader of *An Unfinished Woman* by the time we reach this portrait. Nothing in it comes as a surprise, but as the essay swings between events of his life, and his illness and death, it also sums up the relationship between these two close but separate individualists.

Hammett once said that any biography she wrote of him would turn out to be "the history of Lillian Hellman with an occasional reference to a friend called Hammett." Actually, the portrait is somewhat more than that, but its subject is a relationship rather than a man. Hellman is her old loving/irritable self, able to tolerate just so much intimacy. And she is still the pupil, learning about herself and her craft from this tough disciplinarian and teacher. Hammett was a radical, not only politically, but in the sense that he had to go to the root of things. Throughout the memoirs we watch him help Lillian cut through her self-deceptions, even the well-meaning ones. Under his eyes she could never get away with undeserved self-righteousness.

The essay begins—more or less—with Hammett's illness before his death, then flashes back to their first meeting and the early years, highlighting remembered events in between (with no attempt to "keep books" of them all), and ends with the final illness. The first years were happy and creative, then became sad when his drinking got out of control; then more stable in 1948 when he stopped drinking altogether. It is during this period, from 1948 through the McCarthy years and his imprisonment in 1951, that Hammett emerges in her portrait as a figure of incorruptible integrity; a stubborn hero and patriot. He fought in two wars out of conviction; and found a kind of personal fulfillment in the army —just as some of Hellman's male characters do in the plays. Even his jail term fulfilled a need for him—he remembered the challenge of it, forgetting the deprivation and the illness.

The portrait of Hammett as a public figure, as the idealist, the disciplined writer, then recluse and eclectic reader, the invalid and beloved friend, is multi-dimensional and moving—but not as deeply so as the sections on Helen and Sophronia; or the portrait of "Julia" to emerge in *Pentimento*. Those essays are cries from the soul. "Oh, Sophronia, it's you I want back always. . . ." There is a sense of helpless emotional entanglement with the images of these women—they speak of need, pain, dependence. The essay on Hammett is more rational: it calls up the image of him as the generous good companion, the bulwark, teacher, sometime lover, almost husband. He never liked Helen—or Parker for that matter— as Hellman's father never liked Sophronia: a rival is a rival, acknowledged or not.

The thought of Hammett comes back to Hellman in

conscious recollection as "the most interesting man I've ever met. I laugh at what he did say, amuse myself with what he might say, and even this many years later, speak to him, often angry that he still interferes with me, still dictates the rules." The hot-headed student remembers the cool teacher. But the image of the strong dark mother moves in and out of dreams, day and night, with the tides of consciousness throughout a lifetime.

7

○○○

Pentimento

The title of *Pentimento* is a term from painting: it alludes to the fact that as paint on canvas ages, an earlier painting or parts of one may show through. The artist has "re-pented" of his first effort and painted over it at a later time. In Hellman's words,

> Perhaps it would be well to say that the old conception, re-placed by a later choice, is a way of seeing and seeing again.
>
> That is all I mean about the people in this book. The paint has aged now and I wanted to see what was there for me once, what is there for me now.

Like Henry James, she wanted to "evoke the image and repaint the scene" in past and present time. But in a recent interview, Hellman acknowledged her awareness of fictional or theatrical form in the portraits: "I wouldn't have chosen the people I chose without a feeling for fic-tion, some belief that what I was writing about was interesting or dramatic."[1]

The memoir form, of course, has supplied Hellman with the leeway for commentary and speculation that could not take place on the realistic stage, in a well-made play. She can be more cavalier with time and the sequence of events—moving backward and forward with associa-tions; interrupting an action at a crucial point for sus-pense, as well as commentary. But these essays are still such stuff as plays (or movies) are made on. Four are

portraits: "Bethe," "Willy," "Julia," and "Arthur W. A.
Cowan." The chapter on theater is the exception to the
fictional or play form in that it consists of a series of
brief "pictures, portraits, mementoes" related to Hellman's
plays. The last long essay, "Turtle," is also dramatic, and
in it Hellman returns explicitly to the theme of injury and
survival. She concludes with a brief, short-story epilogue,
"Pentimento," which takes us back to Hammett's death
and Helen's.

The essay "Helen," in *An Unfinished Woman*, was the
strongest link between that book and *Pentimento*. Its
structure is that of a screen play, and its theme, questioning as it did the ways of love in the ways of Helen, il-
lustrated Richard Poirier's concept of "emotional range-
finding." Throughout *Pentimento* we watch Hellman
trying to define her relationships, in the past and the
present, to the people and events in the portraits. Such
"range-finding" is predicated on an inquiry into the nature of love. The old anger and rebellion are still there,
of course, but they now clearly represent the other faces
of love—jealousy and the fear of losing love, coupled
with a fear of love itself. Hellman's deepest lessons about
love were learned from women—Sophronia and Helen,
Hannah and Jenny (her New Orleans aunts), and now,
in addition to the others, but not supplanting them, Bethe
and "Julia."

"Bethe," like all the portraits, has two strands of
plot—the story of Bethe, and the story of Lillian. The
Bethe plot is a tale of adult love played against a backdrop of poverty and violence. But the education of Lillian
by Bethe and her lover, and by Lillian's aunts, Hannah
and Jenny, constitutes the major plot and unifying action
or purpose of this "play." Lillian learns about two kinds
of love: Eros, or sexual love, with its powerful influence
on personality, from Bethe; and agape, or charitable
Christian love, with its lesson in humility, from her aunts.

The portrait opens with a retrospective prologue,

comparable to the brief introductory chapters before the major essays in *An Unfinished Woman*. The narrative proper begins with Hellman's memory of Bethe as a "tall, handsome woman in her late thirties." She had been brought to this country from Germany by wealthy cousins, the Bowmans, who were also Hellman's distant cousins. The Bowmans hoped that an arranged marriage with Bethe might reform their profligate son, Styrie. But Styrie soon abandoned his wife and went back to his old habits; by way of gambling and unpaid debts, he became the object of a Mafia contract. His violent fate at their hands is understated—as is violence throughout the tale. The understatement only adds to the shock: "Styrie was found clinging to the fire escape with his right hand because his left hand was lying on the ground."

But Styrie is no hero, and his final disappearance is only the preface to Bethe's liaison with a mafioso named Arneggio, who is destined to be butchered—literally—in a gang war. Before the murder, however, the teen-age Lillian, on her six-month visit to New Orleans, seeks out Bethe, whom she finds mysterious and fascinating. During a lunch with Bethe in an Italian restaurant, Lillian becomes aware of the love between her and Arneggio, feels excluded and jealous, and storms out of the restaurant in a temper, typical of the adolescent runaway in *An Unfinished Woman*.

Lillian's family enter the Bethe plot, by virtue of their disapproval of Bethe's "common-law marriage," as they call it, and by her aunts' fears for Lillian's safety. Their fears are justified when, on the day after the murder of Arneggio, the police catch Lillian, who is looking for Bethe, at the site of the murder. The child and her aunts are summoned to the police station and questioned. When the police insist on an explanation from Lillian of her presence at the scene of the murder she can only answer, in a state of trembling panic, "I don't know. I read about Mr. Arneggio last night. Love, I think, but I'm not sure."

The aunts persuade Lillian to stay away from Bethe, and she interprets this to mean that the family have rejected their cousin—have turned their backs on Bethe in time of trouble. To Lillian this is immoral—un–Christian.

Years later, after her divorce, and at the start of her liaison with Hammett, Lillian returns to visit her aunts, still nursing her resentment at their supposed rejection of Bethe, and defensive, now, at the probability that they will reject her too because of her own "common-law marriage."

She tells her aunts:

"I know that you will not approve of my living with a man I am not married to, but that's the way it's going to be."

"How do you know that," said Jenny, "how do you know the difference between fear and approve?"

"Because you deserted, sorry, you gave Bethe up, when she loved a way you didn't like."

But this twenty-five year old Lillian is mistaken on two counts: the real hangups about "the way Bethe loved" are not her aunts' but her own; and the shallow, unforgiving moral code is not theirs but hers. The aunts are hurt by her accusations, and reveal that they have always secretly befriended Bethe; had sacrificed to give her financial help during all the trouble. But they had kept their loyalty and charity to themselves. Here, as elsewhere, Hellman half-mocks her own persistent religiosity and "the high-class moral theory stage, from which I have never completely emerged." She has learned her lesson in agape from Hannah and Jenny, and that high-class morality of hers has taken a blow in the process.

The lessons about eros, however, are harder to learn, more complicated and ambiguous. Hellman had long felt that she somehow owed her relationship with Hammett to her knowledge of Bethe's love for Arneggio. But she is never sure whether that was a good thing or not. The closing scene of "Bethe" suggests that conflicts about love and sex that plagued Lillian at fifteen, still torment her at twenty-five.

After their revelation, the aunts take Lillian to see Bethe in her shack on the edge of town. The next day Lillian feels that she must return alone to talk to Bethe. But as she approaches the site of the cabin, she panics, turns and runs, suddenly coming to a swamp. "I heard things jump in the swamp and I remember thinking I must be sick without feeling sick, feverish without fever." When at last she finds a path out of the swamp, it leads directly to Bethe's house. In the yard stands Bethe, naked, hanging clothes on the line. Lillian pauses to admire the proportions of Bethe's figure, and Bethe, hearing the sound of the "wet, ugly, soil" of the swamp beneath Lillian, tries to cover herself with her hands.

The episode is a mixture of ugliness and beauty, revulsion and attraction. If there is a consistent pattern of symbolism in the essay as a whole, I have missed it; but this adventure is certainly recorded in the manner of Hawthorne. Bethe is a Hawthornesque Eve, after the fall —a sort of Hester Prynne, blossoming in a clearing at the edge of the dangerous swamp of sexuality. Lillian cries out, "It was you who did it! I would not have found it without you. Now what good is it, tell me that?" The reader can only guess what "it" is—presumably love between adults—and at the meaning of what follows. Bethe says nothing, but takes Lillian indoors, and gives her a cup of coffee—which Lillian promptly throws up. But she is not sick, she tells Bethe, "Just the opposite. It was that day in the restaurant, you and Arneggio—" but Bethe silences Lillian with a hand over her mouth.

Bethe seems to be happy enough with the man she now lives with. Hellman never sees her again, but recalls in the last paragraph—as the curtain falls, so to speak— an episode with Hammett when she tried to tell him that "Bethe had a lot to do with him and me." He doesn't understand, or doesn't want to, and in a fit of temper, she drives off to the beach at Montauk, Long Island, in the snow, coming back with a case of the grippe.

All this association of Bethe and Hammett with sickness—or fever—is never clarified completely, but it need not be. Whatever Lillian learned from Bethe would always prove to be upsetting. The forbidden fruit was indigestible.

And what she learned from Hannah and Jenny would always be disquieting, would always remind her of her own self-righteousness. The "first Jewish nun on Prytania Street" is still muttering her penitential prayer, having now reached the phrase, "Jenny, Hannah, and all others forgive me. . . ."

"Willy"

In the portrait of Willy the young Lillian is still trying to fathom adult relationships and to define her own nature. She is less successful here than in "Bethe." The teen-aged Lillian is the same one we've seen before— funny, jealous, prurient, romantic. But her older sister, Lillian a decade later, is incredible.

The territory explored by the fourteen-year-old in "Willy" begins with a closet full of family skeletons— mainly the wealthy Newhouse ones. Willy is Lillian's great-uncle, who is married to her mother's Frenchified aunt, Lily; he is the adventurer who involved the family in the United Fruit Company scandals, including the slaughter of natives in Central America. Ultimately he is caught smuggling weapons into the region to put down a native rebellion. But Willy has such charm and vitality that the teen-aged Lillian thinks of him as glamorous and picaresque, in spite of the opinions of her father and the Hellman aunts that he is a reprobate.

The portrait is rich with suspense and humor as young Lillian collects one gem after another of shocking information about Uncle Willy and his family. She learns that Willy has a Cajun girlfriend in the bayou; he has borrowed money from his wife and never returned it; his wife—Aunt Lily—takes morphine supplied to her by the mulatto chauffeur, who is also her lover. The son, Honey, is well on his way toward the "loony bin" for repeated rape. (But even Honey has enough sense to recognize, eventually, that his mother and her lover became characters in *Toys in the Attic*.)

Lillian has first-hand experience with Honey's sexual compulsions, and avoids rape—somehow typically—by sneezing. But most of her knowledge about the goings-on in Willy's family comes from her friend, the old ex-slave, Caroline Ducky, who lives in the attic and does "fine sewing." Her character is sharp, earthy, funny; she sees through all her white people, serving as a chorus, commenting on the action, and punctuating her comments with her favorite—and often appropriate—expletive, "shit."

Caroline Ducky likes Willy and befriends him in his war with the rest of the family, although she tells Lillian, "He ain't no man of God," and crosses herself. This, in a way, becomes Lillian's own attitude, here and later. When Willy invites her—at fourteen—to go with him on a hunting and fishing trip to the bayou, and when, on the way, he buys her boots and other supplies, including twenty-four handkerchiefs, she is ecstatic and falls in love with him. The ecstasy continues during most of the adventure, but turns to rage when she discovers that the Cajun mistress is very real and very intimate with Willy. After nursing her hurt at rejection, and furious at herself for being jealous, Lillian runs out of the bayou (as she did out of the restaurant and the swamp in "Bethe") and hitches a ride back to the city.

The Willy plot of this tale is beautifully done: Hellman draws unforgettable contrasts between Willy's two "families," the New Orleans decadents in their immaculate, pseudo-elegant house, and the Cajun hunters

and fishermen in that rambling, filthy shack in the bayou.
The bayou itself excites with its danger and seductive
beauty. But the Lillian plot—her pilgrim's progress toward maturity—lacks a clear direction.

Lillian's love for Willy is perfectly convincing as an
adolescent crush (or the stirrings of "perberty" as Hellman once called it), but here Hellman takes it seriously.
Commenting in her own voice she says:

I was not ever to fall in love very often, but certainly this
was the first time and I would like to think I learned from it.
But the mixture of ecstasy as it clashed with criticism of
myself and the man was to be repeated all my life, and the
only thing that made the feeling for Uncle Willy different
was the pain of that first recognition: not of love, but of the
struggles caused by love; the blindness of a young girl trying
to make simple sexual desire into something more complex,
more poetic, more unreachable.

And years later, when the young girl is a young
woman, Hellman seems to be telling us that Lillian is
still trying to make "simple sexual desire" into something complex and unreachable. Or is it just the opposite?
Is she trying to interpret complex feelings about Uncle
Willy—her need to defend him against her father's family—in terms of sexual desire? The reader can't be sure.
In any case, when Lillian has presumably grown up and
is living with Hammett—who has tried to make her admit her disapproval of Willy's past—she returns to
Hannah's and Jenny's house in New Orleans. She meets
Willy, who now seems old, fat, and sick, and is living in
a fantasy world of non-existent wealth. He is warm and
generous toward her as always, and when she discovers
that he is broke and down on his luck, she agrees to go
with him to Central America on a romantic expedition,
not unlike the original trip to the bayou.

Willy is not painted here as attractive, and it seems
unlikely, to this reader at least, that Lillian would be
swept away when he touched her hand and said, "Any-

way, it's time you and I finished what we started. Come on." But she is, and all that stops her is her aunts' disgust and Hammett's remark, when she calls to tell him of her plans, that she need not call him when she returns. "I'm not crazy about women who sleep with murderers." The stubborn, rebellious Lillian we have known before would have gone with Willy just because of such an ultimatum. But this time her feelings are too mixed, and she flies back to Los Angeles. But she gets even by not calling Dash. (He finds out that she is there and calls her and there is a reconciliation.)

Ambiguity and conflict are one thing; silliness is another. Hellman says she would like to think she learned from the Willy affair, but for the reader, the evidence is against her. The literary failure here may lie in her technique of "half-mocking" herself and others. When she tried it in the plays, audiences often missed the point —as in the character of Alexandra in *The Little Foxes*. When Hellman's view is clear, the characters are clear: we make no mistake about the adolescent Lillian and the young Uncle Willy. But they are the "pentimento," the underlying images which come through so strongly that they obliterate the more recent portrait; and that one— of an adult Lillian and an aging Willy—becomes hazy, and a bit smudged.

"Julia"

Hellman is as certain of her relationship to Julia, the "beloved friend" of the next portrait, as she is uncertain of that between herself and great-uncle Willy. In "Julia" there is no muddle, no ambivalence or guesswork. Here Hellman's touch is sure, and she is candid in the way that our liberated times allow her to be. The "Lillian" and "Julia" strands of plot are now inextricably interwoven with the "Lillian-Julia" relationship; the image of Julia as a person and an influence stirs at the root of feeling—

somewhere beneath consciousness—as do those of Sophronia, Helen, Hannah, and Jenny; more deeply than that of Bethe or the male subjects of the portraits in *Pentimento*.

The incident around which "Julia" is constructed occurred in 1937, when Hellman smuggled Julia's $50,000 across the German border, to ransom antifascists. The episode is interrupted at a crucial moment in the action by a long flashback into Hellman's childhood, and a forward flash to the 1970s. Then the tale of the Berlin adventure is resumed and concluded. I have told the facts of the story in the biographical preface, above. The essence of "Julia," however, is not in that plot line, but in the Lillian-Julia relationship, seen then and seen now, by the speaker, "Lillian," whose image this time becomes Hellman's own.

The friendship began in New York, when both girls were about twelve, and Lillian's year was divided between New Orleans and New York. Julia was the daughter of a wealthy family and would come into a fortune of her own. To Lillian, Julia was always the intellectual superior, mentor, and teacher; later to become a model, like Hammett, of the committed radical whom Hellman could never be. Julia was also the more sophisticated of the two girls, acknowledging with restraint and tact whatever was sexual in the young Lillian's adoration. As Hellman says, the love she had for Julia was "too strong and too complicated to be defined as only the sexual yearnings of one girl for another. And yet certainly that was there." As the two grew up and followed separate careers, they corresponded and saw each other now and then. In 1933-1934 when Julia was studying medicine in Vienna and had been accepted as a student by Freud, Lillian was living with Dashiell Hammett and was working on *The Children's Hour*. In correspondence Lillian asked Julia what she thought of the title of that play, and was hurt that Julia forgot to answer the question and continued in her letters to warn against the terrors of Nazism, and the coming holocaust. That message did not really get through to Lillian until she had seen Julia's own torture and death at the hands of the Nazis.

Julia's martyrdom made her another symbol of the paradoxical affirmation of life in the face of death, the "survival" of the courageous spirit, in spite of bodily mutilation, that Hellman so often celebrates in the memoirs. Julia's example, moreover, had called forth the best in Lillian—the delivery of the money demanded a nerve and courage she never knew she had. Even after death, Julia forced adulthood on her friend. Lillian had to act alone, in place of the family that disclaimed the dead, as they had the living, Julia.

And then there was the question of Julia's illegitimate child, another gesture toward life in the face of imminent death. Julia had called the child Lilly; but had never named the father, and the child was never found. But an ironic web of relationships leads Hellman to the angry realization of the father's identity and of still another terrible injustice done her friend. In a recent interview Hellman said that she had changed the names and places in "Julia" to avoid a lawsuit from Julia's family— still living. "I was really saying they had never wanted to find her baby."[2]

Hellman's anger in "Julia" is, for the most part, that of an adult. It is directed at real evil and injustice—is not just a function of purely personal jealousy or injury. She throws one typical Hellman tantrum when she slaps the face of a friend's drunken brother, for making an off-color remark about her relationship with Julia. But we discover gradually, as Lillian does, that the scandal-mongering "friend" is about to marry the father of Julia's child.

Anger, in this essay, is all that makes the suffering bearable for both Hellman and the reader. Julia was the only person who appreciated the value of Lillian's anger as a motivating force; as readers we see in it the alternative

to Lillian's dissolution—the preservative of her sanity.
When Lillian tries to tell Julia's family about her death
and is turned away from the house; when she bends over
the slashed face of the dead friend; and when she brings
the unclaimed body home for cremation instead of a
hero's funeral—Hellman's anger becomes the banner of
her own survival.

"Julia" is the high point of *Pentimento*. All its elements—plot, character, human and physical ambience—
work together to produce exciting drama, and an exciting,
if rather conventionally constructed, film. It may be
instructive, however, to read the comments of the actresses
who play Lillian and Julia.

Jane Fonda: "It's about the relationship between
two women. It's not neurotic or sexually aberrant, it's
just about two friends who care about each other tre-
mendously, who are interested in each other's growth.
There isn't any gossip or jealousy.

"The fact is that it's about a woman who is a real
heroine. It is very important to make movies about women
who grow and become ideological human beings and
totally committed people. We have to begin to put that
image into the mass culture."

Vanessa Redgrave: "Julia is very much like the title
of the book, she is an obscured character whom you can
just catch through the varnish and smoke, but you only
perceive outlines and contours. The story is really about
Lillian Hellman and how she felt about her friend. . . .
It is not remotely a political film. It is about the friendship between two women. It is not about events. The question of why tens of thousands like Julia were defeated is
not even dealt with."[3]

"Arthur W. A. Cowan"

The Broadway theater, which to Hellman had represented
hard work and struggle as she developed an instinctive

talent, seemed remote at the time of the writing of *Pentimento*. The chapter called "Theater" is a collection of anecdotes, gossip, "chatter of failure and success," as Hellman puts it. Most of the relevant or important material has been presented above in connection with the plays or the biography. But the "Theater" chapter serves as a bridge between the years of "Julia," the late thirties, and those of the portrait of Arthur W. A. Cowan, the sixties.

Cowan was a wealthy lawyer and longtime friend of Hellman. Both his life and death were something of a mystery—he created conflicting images of himself, and the truth never quite came through to his friends. In the retrospect of the memoirs, Hellman sees him as a kind of sad curiosity, under all his flair and mystery—a good potential character for a play like *The Autumn Garden*.

Arthur lives high and gives generously, even to liberal causes, although his own politics typify the worst in American conservatism. When he flaunts his opinionated bigotry at his liberal friends they find him "unbearable," but they know that he is also insecure and sensitive. He is driven to test people's responses to him—his own type of "range-finding." At one point, when Arthur fancies that he has been rejected by Lillian—whom he courts on and off—he retaliates by accusing her of caring only for his money. This is a sore point for her—the accusation that she could be bought. She gives way to one of her rages, "without control, murderous," and strikes out verbally at Arthur's sensitive areas—his looks, his aging, his sexual prowess—and he is crushed. It is not until much later, near the end of his life, that she watches him go to pieces in unprovoked, unreasonable rage aimed at no one in particular. "Something had gone wrong with Arthur, now forever." She was no longer angry; would never "pay him the compliment of anger" again.

If Hellman saw any similarity between her own rages and Cowan's she does not say so; we have no hint that she ever identifies with him. Both before and after his crackup she considered him a "man of unnecessary things," constantly driven to cover his inadequacies with a passion for luxurious novelty—new cars, new houses, new women. But Lillian is to be reminded by Helen (her black sibylline superego) that she is too unsympathetic to Arthur. Helen has accepted a gift of money and a too-small but expensive coat from Cowan, for *his* sake. She tells Lillian, "He means no harm. You never understood that." It is Helen, too, who senses that Cowan's death is imminent: "He's doing what we all must do, come soon, come late, getting ready for the summons, and you ought to put out a hand."

Hellman says she had heard "that kind of talk before" and does not want to listen, but she has to. For Dash is dying in the house—Arthur Cowan would live to settle his estate—and Helen herself was to answer the summons before long.

"Turtle"

The two final chapters, "Turtle" and "Pentimento," bring together the two major themes of the memoirs, survival and love. In *An Unfinished Woman* and in earlier chapters of this book, Hellman had continually questioned the meanings of those terms. Now they become almost synonymous. The simple human conclusion Hellman comes to is that while all our instincts of self-preservation, and all our longings propel us toward a belief in survival after death for ourselves and others, the only experience we have of such "resurrection" is that of the living—the remembrance of the dead by those who loved them. Both these chapters continue with questioning, floundering, ambivalence, sidetracking, but this is where we come out in the end, although Hellman does not say so directly. She almost never lectures; she dramatizes.

"Turtle" is the macabre, bloody—rather than "black"

—comedy, of a snapping turtle that stubbornly survived its own "death." The event goes back in time to Pleasantville, on the farm, when Hammett and Hellman try to kill a turtle that has injured one of the poodles. But even after the turtle's head has been almost severed—is hanging by a strip of skin—the reflexes keep functioning, and overnight the turtle leaves a trail of blood from the stove, on which it was supposed to be cooked, to the path leading to the lake from which it came. Lillian feels that the turtle has earned its life, and deserves a decent burial out of respect for its struggle, rather than to be cooked and eaten. Hammett resists, as always, what he considers childish superstition; he is himself an ex-Catholic and does not want to be badgered about the significance of the turtle's death, either by Lillian or by Helen, the cook, who is a Catholic convert.

Hammett's opinion becomes, in the essay, a vehicle for Hellman's "half-mockery" of herself and of her earnest but jejune philosophical questions: "What is life? Stuff like that." Hammett refuses to be a party to a funeral for a turtle he had planned to make into soup, and Lillian, with the help of a bottle of whiskey, buries the snapper herself. But some animal digs it up, and Hammett seems to have the last word when he reburies the bones under a wooden sign reading, "My first turtle is buried here. Miss Religious L.H."

This is the last word in the essay, but the real last word is Hellman's "first word" in a prologue to "Turtle," sounding a familiar motif. She has gone swimming from a boat in the sound at Martha's Vineyard. The tide separates her from her boat, and she thinks she is helplessly drifting out to sea—until she washes against a piling of a large pier. As she clings to the piling, she recalls a conversation with Hammett four days after the death of the turtle.

"You understood each other," she said. "He was a survivor and so are you. But what about me?" Hammett did not want to answer, but finally said, "I don't know, maybe you are, maybe not. What good is my opinion?" (Probably he means that no one can judge the significance of a survival except the survivor.) To the reader, Hellman adds, "Holding to the piling, I was having a conversation with a man who had been dead five years about a turtle who had been dead for twenty-six." Neither of them is dead to Hellman. Both survived, if nowhere else, in the memoirs.

So, also, with Helen, the subject of the portrait by that title in *An Unfinished Woman*—now seen again and "repainted" in the final chapter called "Pentimento." And, as usual, the essay is also a look—and a look again—at Lillian. The chapter begins immediately after the death of Hammett, when Hellman and Helen have moved to Cambridge, where the writer is to be teaching at Harvard. Hammett was supposed to have come with them, and to have stayed at a nearby nursing home. His death has been so recent, his presence so immediate, that Hellman finds herself each night walking to the nursing home, where Hammett should have been. Helen is worried about her, and she and a talented student, Jimsie, whom Helen has befriended, keep an eye on Lillian, sometimes following her on her nightly walks.

The subplot of this drama—or screenplay—has to do with the friendship between Helen and Jimsie, and with Jimsie's career. But the major plot, from the opening scene to the final curtain or fadeout, is the relationship of Lillian Hellman to "her dead"—to echo the protagonist of Henry James's tale, "The Altar of the Dead." Everybody in the book, except Jimsie, she says, is dead. "I don't want to write about Jimsie; that isn't the point here and he wouldn't like it."

But Jimsie helps her make her final point in the essay. The sequence begins when she goes to look at the nursing home for one last time and finds that Jimsie has followed her. She gazes at the building, apparently trying to come to terms with her feelings, and says aloud the word, "pentimento." When Jimsie asks what she means the only reply he receives is a scolding, "Don't follow me again, Jimsie, I don't like it."

Then Helen dies. Time passes, and Jimsie, who a few years before had taken Helen's body to South Carolina for burial, contacts Hellman in New York. They talk first about his life and his values—those of a confused, resigned, ex-radical of the 1960s student movement. They talk about Helen, and Jimsie calls her "that great, big, fine lady, doing her best in the world." Helen had once given him a coat. When he told her he could not take "presents from a working lady" she had slapped his face. Hellman said,

"You once told me you didn't understand about like or dislike."

He said, "I loved Helen."

"Too bad you never told her so. Too late now."

"I told it to her," he said, "The night I looked up your word, pentimento."

This is more than just a too-neat way to conclude the book. Jimsie understands that in life, love may not have a second chance to express itself. The only second chance is in the "pentimento" of the memory of those who survive. We remember or repaint what we want to, never mind the reality. Helen understood that, too. She had tried to talk to Hellman about death and about Hammett: "You go stand in front of that place because you think you can bring him back. Maybe he don't want to come back, and maybe you don't. . . ." she breaks off. Hellman adds, "It was a long time before I knew what she had been about to say. . . ." This must have been that Lillian actually—unconsciously—preferred the dim picture from the past, the "pentimento," to the more real and recent image of Dash.

At the end of the portrait of Hammett, Hellman had

said that she did not want to end her book on an elegiac note. And for all the talk of death and aging in the memoirs they are not sad, or morbid, or even nostalgic. Hellman's devotion is to life—to questioning what it means, if anything, and what we must be, or do, or endure in order to say we have "survived."

And for all her bad temper, *An Unfinished Woman* and *Pentimento* are not consistently angry books: anger is intrinsic to survival, in her terms, but so also is love. She is not talking about "romance"—that out-of-date term is for the "lady writers" of her generation. She means human communication and acceptance; faulty, partial they may be, but they give life its hope and sense of adventure.

8

Scoundrel Time

Compared to the other memoirs, *Scoundrel Time* (1976), is a minor literary performance that elicited a major political controversy. The book is a slight one, only 155 pages, of which thirty-four are introduction by Garry Wills. The narrative itself is brief, with remembered sidelights and flashbacks. Hellman said that it had originally been part of *An Unfinished Woman*, and then "of a much longer book I've been working on for some time," but her editor persuaded her to publish it separately[1]—a wise decision.

The "time" of the title, of course, was the period of the late forties and early fifties when a "Red scare" resulted in the investigations by, among other bodies, the House Un-American Activities Committee. After enduring what were sometimes inquisitorial hearings, many people who were suspected of being communists or fellow travelers were blacklisted or cited for contempt of Congress, which could result in a prison sentence. The "scoundrels" of the title resembled the characters of Hellman's plays: they included not only the active villains, the "despoilers," like Senator McCarthy himself, but those whom Hellman accused of being *his* fellow-travellers—the "bystanders" who supported the "witch-hunt" by failing to attack McCarthy or to defend or rescue those like herself whose reputations and fortunes had been damaged. In fact,

147

Hellman is harder on these than she is on the senator and the various committees.

The elliptical and often ambiguous style of the other memoirs was, in those books, a legitimate medium for describing the author's personal reactions to life. Most of the characters in those books were dead; names and identities could be changed and shifted to protect the living. Moreover, those memoirs were intended as artifact, not history; accuracy was not the point. But many of the people accused in *Scoundrel Time* of being bystanders to villainy are still alive, and Hellman attacked them by name. They fought—and are still fighting—back. Their charges are based on alleged inaccuracies and omissions in Hellman's facts, and on her stance as the lonely truth-speaker.

As a literary performance, the book has a certain understated charm. It is discursive and anecdotal, less tightly constructed than the memoir chapters I have called dramatic tales. The tone is less that of anger than of disappointment and weariness that Hellman's "old, respected friends" could have been parties to injustice. But she still constructs a series of dramatic confrontations—somewhat episodic now, and sliding forward and backward in time—to build toward the climax, her appearance before the House Un-American Activities Committee in May of 1952. And in spite of her sad or wry disillusionment, the old cantankerous, hot-tempered Lillian is still the protagonist—the Southern kid now grown up, who took her values from Sophronia, including "my own liking for black people." Sophronia "was an angry woman and she gave me anger, an uncomfortable, dangerous, and often useful gift." Even in the famous letter to the Committee Hellman echoed Sophronia's plea to her not to go through life making trouble for people.

Ah, but then the irony! The first dramatic confrontation, resulting in a flareup of the famous temper, came with the serving of the summons to appear before the

Committee—served by "an over-respectable looking black man, a Sunday deacon." He politely handed Miss Hellman the envelope; she opened it and read the subpoena. "I said, 'Smart to choose a black man for this job. You like it?' and slammed the door." A white Southerner—some white Southerners—might understand her sense of betrayal. But one can only hope that this particular clerk, doing his job, understood that there was nothing racist or personal in this white-lady's rudeness. However.

After the summons, Hellman leads us through further confrontations, some friendly, some not; some spiced with anger or scorn, or humor. She had conferred about her case with lawyer friends and they recommended Joseph Rauh, a distinguished liberal attorney, who had been Chairman of the Executive Committee of Americans for Democratic Action since 1947. Rauh agreed to support her position that she was willing to tell the Committee whatever they wanted to know about her own activities, but was not willing to discuss the activities of anyone else. She and Rauh drafted the letter to the Committee, stating that she did not wish to take the Fifth Amendment, but understood that she might have to do so rather than to name other people, and "bring bad trouble" to them.

Five days before the hearing she went to Washington and holed up alone in a hotel without telling Hammett or her lawyers where she was. The next day she went shopping to build her morale, then called Hammett. During the following days she killed time—went to the museum, did more shopping, and bought an expensive designer dress and appropriate accessories for her "day in court." Through her descriptions of the sleepless nights, retrospective fears, worries, and conflicts, up to the last minute before the hearing, Hellman feeds the reader's anticipation of the courtroom scene.

Rauh was happy when the press crowded into the room. The letter had been refused in writing by the Com-

mittee the day before the hearing: witnesses could not
stipulate the terms under which they would testify. Hellman knew that she would have to take the Fifth Amendment as others had, or testify in full. The questioning
began with her past in Hollywood, and included the
accusation by Martin Berkeley (see biography, above)
that she had attended a Communist Party meeting in his
home in 1937. At this point in the questioning, Hellman
asked to have her letter to the Committee reconsidered.
The chairman, for clarification, ordered the letter read—
aloud—into the record (as well as the letter of refusal
from the Committee). Joseph Rauh was prepared with
mimeographed copies of Hellman's letter on hand, which
he passed out to the press. As the questioning continued,
and she was forced to take the Fifth on some questions,
the members of the press were reading the letter. It was
then that, according to Hellman, a voice from the press
gallery said aloud, "Thank God somebody finally had the
guts to do it."

Hellman said that this was probably the best minute
of her life. It was the high point in her account of the
hearing. She keeps it from sounding too self-congratula-
tory by her customary self-deprecation. "Many people
have said they liked what I did, but I don't much, and if
I hadn't worried about rats in jail, and such. . . ." In
any case, the Committee gave up the questioning and she
was excused from further attendance. Publication of the
letter made her a heroine to many people—indeed, the
following week, when she spoke the narration for Marc
Blitzstein's opera, *Regina*, based on *The Little Foxes*, she
was greeted with "thunderous applause" and a standing
ovation.

This is the essential narrative of *Scoundrel Time*.
It is surrounded by related memories. The hearing was
followed by the sad departure from the farm, told with a
retrospective account—not always kind—of Hellman's

acquaintance with Henry Wallace, the Progressive Party's presidential candidate, for whom she had campaigned. Then the action moves forward to 1953 when she went to Rome to do a movie for Alexander Korda. (Although she was blacklisted, it was possible for her to work outside of Hollywood.) After the movie failed to materialize, Hellman was shadowed by an American agent of the CIA. To her, that was adding insult to recent injury, and convinced her beyond doubt that there was a close connection between the national fear of communism in the fifties, on which a McCarthy could thrive, and the same fear that in later times would lead to CIA surveillance of private citizens and would be related to Watergate, "dirty tricks," and the Vietnam war.

The logic of these connections is not, however, universally acknowledged, or made clear in *Scoundrel Time*. Hellman has always insisted that politics and history are not her game; her commitments, apparently, have always been dependent upon personal experience and loyalties—to "Julia," Hammett, Raya Kopelev (her Russian guide)—rather than upon ideology or comprehensive knowledge of historical fact. Hellman's leftist leanings reflected not only her admiration of "radicals, domestic and foreign," but also her awareness of economic injustice—sharpened by her own guilt about the big money she made during the Depression from *The Children's Hour* and her screenwriting. But she left the broader aspects of history and politics to the specialists, like those who wrote her introductions: Garry Wills to the American edition of *Scoundrel Time*, and James Cameron to the English edition.

Hellman may be neither historian nor political scientist, nor logician, but her book and Wills' inflammatory introduction brought into focus a deep and irreconcilable conflict in American views of history. The conflict is not simply between the right and the left, but between factions of the intellectuals on the left. It goes back to the 1930s when news began to leak through the iron curtain of the crimes of the Stalinist regime in Russia—the purges, the mock trials, the mass imprisonments. Many Marxist and Leninist intellectuals in America abandoned the pro-Communist position when it became clear that Stalin, like Hitler, posed a real threat to world freedom.

Other intellectuals, however, considered that threat to be much over-rated. They held that the Western military-industrial establishment was the real destroyer of liberty; that in America, the effort of this establishment to perpetuate itself has led to unjust wars abroad and capitalistic abuses of individual freedom at home. In the battle over *Scoundrel Time* this view was supported by the revisionist historians, who held with Garry Wills (himself an ex-hardline-conservative) that it was American aggression under Truman, rather than Russian aggression under Stalin, that, by way of the Cold War, McCarthyism, and Korea, had led to Nixon and Vietnam. Hellman's own support of this position in *Scoundrel Time* is done through assumptions, suggestions, and allusions to her own experience rather than through the citation of facts. These were plentifully available in the publications of her own Committee for Public Justice, and might have strengthened her position.

But Hellman has always been a bit dogmatic in her value judgements—especially if she has been personally offended—and sometimes is carried away by the opportunity to air an old grudge. So she let fly in *Scoundrel Time*—sometimes masking her anger under the tone, as I have said, of sorrowful disillusionment with old friends who belonged to the intellectual anticommunist left. These friends included the writers and editors of most of the literary journals, such as *Partisan Review* and *Commentary*, who, Hellman said, had not published articles attacking McCarthy or defending those people who were attacked by him; Hollywood writers like Clifford Odets and Elia Kazan who became "friendly witnesses"; anticommunist intellectual leaders and critics, like Diana and Lionel Trilling.

These, and many others, were the targets of her fire, but Hellman so scattered her shot that her book seemed to some critics to be snobbish and antisemitic, or at least, in the words of *The Economist* "offensively patrician."[2]

Simply, then and now, I feel betrayed by the nonsense I had believed. I had no right to think that American intellectuals were people who would fight for anything if so doing would injure them; they have very little history that would lead to that conclusion. Many of them found in the sins of Stalin Communism—and there were plenty of sins and plenty that for a long time I mistakenly denied—the excuse to join those who should have been their hereditary enemies. Perhaps that, in part, was the penalty of nineteenth-century immigration. The children of timid immigrants are often remarkable people: energetic, intelligent, hardworking; and often they make it so good that they are determined to keep it at any cost.

When *Scoundrel Time* first came out in April of 1976 the reviews (with some exceptions) were ecstatic, and the book sailed through the spring and summer on the best-seller list for twenty-three weeks. But by the fall, Nathan Glazer had answered in *Commentary*,[3] William Phillips, in and for the *Partisan Review*.[4] Diana Trilling had had a book rejected by Little, Brown and Company because of her attack on one of its authors (Hellman)[5] and Irving Howe had answered Hellman in *Dissent*.[6] That winter the *London Times Literary Supplement* entered the fray with Richard Mayne's critique of the British edition, followed in subsequent weeks by letters pro and con.[7]

But the salvo in which war was really declared, was fired in *The New York Times* of October 3 with a review by Hilton Kramer commenting on the current interest in the period of the House Un-American Activities Committee hearings, as seen in two new movies (*The Front*

and *Hollywood on Trial*) and *Scoundrel Time*. Kramer
attacked Hellman's position and that of the revisionist
historians.

In the next two issues of the Sunday *Times*, sixteen
letters and two more columns of commentary on the
subject appeared. Opinion was divided much as I have
described the two positions above. On the whole, Hellman
came out very well; the opposition to Kramer, accusing
him of distorting history, wrote more and longer letters.
The quarrel has kept Hellman and her views in the spot-
light, and will no doubt add to public interest in any
additional memoirs to come. But her counter-attackers in
the *Scoundrel Time* debate have denied her allegations
and seriously challenged some of her facts, her veracity,
and the "persona" of herself that emerges from this book.
The debate, pro and con, still continues—from liberal
magazines, to the right-wing *National Review*, with a
scathing attack by William F. Buckley Jr.;[8] from serious
literary and aesthetic journals, to *Esquire*, with a percep-
tive discussion by Alfred Kazin;[9] it has even extended to
television interviews[10] and news commentary.

The argument against Hellman was perhaps best
summarized by Sidney Hook in the British magazine,
Encounter.[11] Professor Hook pointed out some of her
mistakes in fact and argued that she and her proponents
were either ignorant of the past or lacking in "historical
memory" of the political crimes of Stalinist Communism
—and were banking on a similar lapse of memory in
Hellman's readers. (This was the argument picked up by
Eric Sevareid in his news commentary of April 1, 1977,
reporting on her speech about her political past in her
presentation of Oscar Awards a few days before.)

Hellman's implicit assumption that to be anti-Communist meant to be pro-McCarthy was particularly in-
furiating to people like Diana Trilling. When her book,
We Must March My Darlings was finally published in
the summer of 1977, the passages which persuaded Little,

Brown and Company to turn it down seemed mild, indeed. But Trilling added several pages of notes contradicting Hellman and pointing out mistakes and fallacies in her arguments.[12]

Hellman's defenders on the whole, have not addressed themselves—as her attackers have—to the actual text of *Scoundrel Time.* Some have leaned heavily on argument *ad hominem*: i.e. her character and behavior; others have talked to the political issues raised by the book. Thomas R. Edwards, for example, in his review of Diana Trilling's book, defended Hellman's general position as a liberal and especially "the commitment to pride in self and loyalty to others that made Lillian Hellman's response to persecution so humanly admirable. . ."[13] Revisionist historians, however, have given strong support to Hellman's contention that the intellectuals who were anti-communist were partly responsible for the Cold War and the mentality that would ultimately sacrifice democratic liberties to government surveillance.[14]

But Hellman herself has not answered her opponents in any cogent, credible way. She claims that she was writing her personal story, not history. Some of her hostile critics have called the book "self-serving;" the character of "Lillian" too heroic, too put-upon and almost martyred, considering the comparative extent of her financial losses and persecution. But the readers who made the book a best-seller thought it was a modest understatement of heroism; that the portrait she presents is of a woman who, in evil times, stuck to her own values against odds and under pressure, and won. These values were based on a personal code of justice, decency, and loyalty to ones friends.

Just as she would not name her friends to the Committee, so Hellman did not decline to write an introduction for a friend's book that challenged her own ideological views. The book is Lev Kopelev's *To Be Preserved Forever* (Lippincott, 1977). The author is the husband

of Raya, Hellman's Russian interpreter, guide, and friend
of thirty-odd years. Kopelev, a distinguished scholar and
writer, is a former doctrinaire Stalinist who spent ten
years in Russian prison camps on various trumped-up
charges. But his book is a confession that he had been
deluded by Stalinist Communism and only the long imprisonment could have made him see the truth:

I came to understand that my fate, which had seemed so
senselessly, so undeservedly cruel, was actually fortunate and
just. It was just because I did deserve to be punished—for
the many years I had zealously participated in plundering
the peasants, worshipping Stalin, lying and deceiving myself
in the name of "historical necessity," and teaching others to
believe in lies and to bow before scoundrels.[15]

Thus Kopelev gives confirmation to the judgment of
Hellman's opponents, the American anti-Communist left.
Still, he was a friend—or the husband of a friend—and
she introduced the book with a wary, somewhat sentimental recollection of Raya and Lev. She concluded with
the footnote, "I have written these notes before Kopelev's
book came from the printer. I am thus in no position to
comment on it. But perhaps that is just as well. I set out
to show my respect for the man."[16]

Such a value system as Hellman's, whether in the
plays or the memoirs, with its clearcut criteria of good
and evil, has a reassuring emotional appeal; it makes us
nostalgic for a child's world (where the worst crime is
to tattle on your friends) and for the make-believe world
of fiction and drama, of despoilers and bystanders, where
such a system flourishes. But the adult realm of politics
and history demands complexities of knowledge and fact,
in which value judgments are painfully arrived at. We
must do more than ask Sophronia.

Lillian Hellman's insight is sharpest when it is most
personal and specific. If some of her plays seem dated

now it is probably because of their "well-made," realistic mode and their two-dimensional, good-or-evil characterizations. But three plays (and perhaps others) have had current repertory revivals—*The Autumn Garden, Toys in the Attic,* and *The Children's Hour.* These are the less structured ones, more concerned with psychology than plot, and with moral ambiguity rather than moral definition.

As a memoirist, Hellman was able to present her materials dramatically, without the limitations imposed by the stage. The memoir form allowed, too, for subtlety in the exploration of character; for unanswered questions, and for a certain mysterious quality that evoked a response from readers who knew that mystery for their own.

The personal, the ambiguous, were not appropriate, however, to the politics of *Scoundrel Time,* and Hellman has taken some punishment for that mistake. But she formulated her philosophy of survival when she was fourteen: "If you are willing to take the punishment, you are halfway through the battle."

Lillian Hellman is still producing, still battling, still surviving, still performing. Whatever we may think of her politics or temperament, we must rejoice in the energy, ingenuity, and skill of the performance.

Notes

I. HELLMAN IN HER TIME: A BIOGRAPHICAL PREFACE

1. Rex Reed, *Valentines and Vitriol*, (New York: Delacorte Press, 1977) p. 105.
2. Eric Bentley (ed), *Thirty Years of Treason, Excerpts from Hearings before the House Committee on Un-American Activities 1938-1968*, (New York: The Viking Press, 1971) p. 533.
3. Richard Moody, *Lillian Hellman, Playwright* (New York: Pegasus, 1972) p. 140.
4. Lillian Hellman, *The North Star: A Motion Picture about Some Russian People* (New York: The Viking Press, 1943).
5. Walter Goodman, *The Committee* (New York: Farrar, Straus & Giroux, 1968), p. 187.
6. Typical of this view is that of Nathan Glazer, one of the earliest attackers of *Scoundrel Time*: "I thought then—and I believe now—that the defense of freedom required one to expose the Communist organizers of this meeting, required one to demonstrate the obscenity of speaking of world peace under the auspices of a movement whose leaders ran a huge system of slave camps for dissenters, who extirpated even the most modest efforts at independence of mind, who just about then were executing the leading Jewish poets and writers of Russia (even though these poets and writers had served them well). What was Lillian Hellman doing in

that company?" "An Answer to Lillian Hellman," *Commentary*, 61, (June, 1976) p. 37.

7. Sen. McCarthy (R. Wisc.) made his maiden flight from obscurity to notoriety on the strength of a speech he made in 1950 alleging that the State Department was full of Communists (the number varied between 205 and 57 and "a lot") and that this fact was known to the Secretary of State. The charge—never proved—set off a series of investigations which threatened the reputations and livelihoods of thousands, in and out of government service, and ultimately succeeded in inhibiting two presidents, both of whom despised McCarthy.

8. Walter Goodman, *The Committee* (New York: Farrar, Straus & Giroux, 1968) p. 219.

9. Dr. Jerome Wiesner, "In Celebration of Lillian Hellman: Origins of the CPJ," *CPJ Newsletter* (Spring, 1976) p. 4.

10. Pat Watters and Stephen Gillers, (ed.) *Investigating the FBI*, (Garden City, N.Y.: Doubleday and Company, Inc., 1973)

     Norman Dorsen and Stephen Gillers, (ed.) *None of Your Business: Government Secrecy in America*, (New York: The Viking Press, 1974).

1. HELLMAN'S DRAMATIC MODE— "THE THEATRE IS A TRICK . . ."

1. Thomas Lask, "A Theater Event Called 'I'," *New York Times*, 4 February, 1977, p. C-3. For additional material on Theatricalist drama see John Gassner, *Directions in Modern Theatre and Drama: An Expanded Edition of Form and Idea in Modern Theatre* (New York: Holt, Rinehart, Winston, 1965) and Richard Gilman, *The Making of Modern Drama* (New York: Farrar, Straus & Giroux, 1974).

2. John Russell Taylor, *The Rise and Fall of the Well-Made Play* (New York: Hill and Wang, 1967) pp. 12, 15.

2. Signposts

1. Burns Mantle (ed.), *The Best Plays of 1934-35* (New York: Dodd, Mead & Co., 1935). The statistics above have been compiled, not quoted, from this source.

2. For a fuller listing of plays on homosexuality in the 1920s and 30s see W. David Sievers, *Freud on Broadway* (New York: Hermitage House, 1955) pp. 93-95, 216-219.

3. Manfred Triesch, *The Lillian Hellman Collection at the University of Texas* (Austin, Texas: 1966) A-ld, quoted in Appendix, p. 102. (Hereafter cited as *Hellman Collection-University of Texas*).

4. Brooks Atkinson, "The Play: *The Children's Hour,*" *New York Times* (21 November, 1934) p. 23.

5. Eric Bentley, "Lillian Hellman's Indignation" in *The Dramatic Event: An American Chronicle* (New York: Horizon Press, 1953) pp. 49-52.

6. Christine Doudna, "A Still Unfinished Woman," *Rolling Stone* (24 February, 1977), p. 55.

7. Sam Smiley, *The Drama of Attack* (Columbia: University of Missouri Press, 1972) p. 29.

8. M. Triesch, *Hellman Collection-University of Texas* (Austin: 1966) A- 2b, p. 20.

3. The Despoilers

1. These are described in *Pentimento*; the first eight are available in M. Triesch, *Hellman Collection-University of Texas* (Austin: 1966) A-3c, d, e, f, g, h, i, j, pp. 25-27.

2. Lillian Hellman, "Back of Those Foxes," *New York Times* (26 February, 1939) Sec. 10, p. 1.

3. John Phillips and Anne Hollander, "Lillian Hellman" in *Writers at Work: The 'Paris Review' Interviews,* third series, Intro. Alfred Kazin (New York: The Viking Press, 1967) p. 121.

4. Lillian Hellman, *Pentimento* (New York: Little Brown and Co., 1973) p. 148.

5. George Jean Nathan, "Dour Octopus," *Newsweek*, Vol. 13 (27 February, 1939) p. 36.

6. Elizabeth Hardwick, *"The Little Foxes* Revived," *New York Review of Books*, vol. 9 (21 December, 1967) pp. 4-5.

7. Edmund Wilson, "An Open Letter to Mike Nichols," *New York Review of Books*, vol. 9 (4 January, 1968) p. 32.

8. Brooks Atkinson, "The Play: *Another Part of the Forest*," *New York Times* (21 November, 1946) p. 42:2.

9. Lillian Hellman, "Author Jabs the Critic," *New York Times* (15 December, 1946) sec. 2, p. 3.

10. M. Triesch, *Hellman Collection-University of Texas* (Austin: 1966) p. 40.

11. In the first printing of *Eugene O'Neill and the Tragic Tension* (New Brunswick, New Jersey: Rutgers University Press, 1958), I mistakenly attributed Ezra Mannon's death to the withholding of medicine—as in Horace's—rather than a substitution of poison for the medicine, which takes place in the O'Neill play. Even the two stricken daughters standing by, Lavinia and Alexandra, are similar.

12. Wolcott Gibbs, "This Is It," *The New Yorker*, vol. 17 (12 April, 1941), p. 32.

13. Margaret Harriman, "Miss Lily of New Orleans: Lillian Hellman" in *Take Them Up Tenderly* (New York: Alfred A. Knopf, 1945) p. 104.

4. THE BYSTANDERS

1. M. Triesch, *Hellman Collection-University of Texas* (Austin: 1966) pp. 114-116.

2. Margaret Marshall, "Drama," *The Nation*, vol. 158 (Apr. 22, 1944) p. 495.

3. John Gassner, *Theatre at the Crossroads* (New York: Holt, Rinehart, Winston, 1960) p. 136.

4. John Mason Brown, "A New Miss Hellman," *The Saturday Review*, Vol. 34 (31 March, 1951) p. 27.

5. Harry Gilroy, "Lillian Hellman Drama Foregoes A Villain," *New York Times* (25 February, 1951) sec. 2, p. 1.

6. Ibid.
7. Harold Clurman, "Lillian Hellman's Garden," *The New Republic*, 124 (26 March, 1951) p. 22.
8. Ibid.
9. I shall give these only brief mention here, but for additional comment and bibliography the student should consult the relevant chapters in Richard Moody, *Lillian Hellman, Playwright* (New York: Pegasus, 1972) and Manfred Triesch, *Hellman Collection-University of Texas* (Austin: 1966).
10. Anton Chekhov, *The Selected Letters of Anton Chekhov*, ed. Lillian Hellman, Trans. Sidonie Lederer (New York: Farrar, Straus & Co., 1955).
11. Burt Blechman, *How Much?: A Novel by B. Halpern as told to Burt Blechman.* (New York: I. Obalensky, 1961).
12. Jacob H. Adler, "Miss Hellman's Two Sisters," *Educational Theatre Journal*, 15 (May, 1963) pp. 112, 117.
13. Richard Moody, *Lillian Hellman, Playwright* (New York: Pegasus, 1972) p. 306.
14. Richard G. Stern, "Lillian Hellman on her Plays," *Contact*, Vol. 3 (1959) p. 117.
15. Alan S. Downer, *Recent American Drama* (Minneapolis: University of Minnesota Press, 1961) p. 42.

5. FORM AND THEME IN THE MEMOIRS— "THROUGH THIS TIME AND THAT TIME . . ."

1. Lacey Fosburgh, "Why More Top Novelists Don't Go to Hollywood," *New York Times*, (21 November, 1976) p. 13.
2. Stendhal (Marie-Henri Beyle) *The Life of Henry Brulard*, trans. Jean Stewart and B.C.J.G. Knight (London: The Merlin Press, 1958).

    W. B. Yeats, *The Autobiography of William Butler Yeats* (New York: Macmillan, 1966).

    Henry James, *A Small Boy and Others* (New York: Charles Scribner's Sons, 1913).

    ———, *Notes of a Son and Brother* (New York: Charles Scribner's Sons, 1914).

3. Henry James, *A Small Boy and Others* (New York: Charles Scribner's Sons, 1913) p. 3.
4. Lillian Hellman, "The Land that Holds the Legend of our Lives," *Ladies' Home Journal*, Vol. 81, (Apr. 1964) p. 57.
5. Hersey said that Hellman had "a hidden religious streak but an open hatred of piety." (John Hersey, "Lillian Hellman," *The New Republic*, 175 [18 September, 1976] p. 25).
6. Richard Poirier, "*Pentimento: A Book of Portraits by Lillian Hellman*," *The Washington Post*, Book Review Section (16 September, 1973) p. 4.

6. An Unfinished Woman

1. Nora Ephron, "Lillian Hellman Walking, Cooking, Writing, Talking," *New York Times Book Review* (23 September, 1973) p. 2.
2. Two of Hellman's earliest publications ridicule "modern" (1933) overemphasis on sexual expression and freedom. (Lillian Hellman, "I Call Her Mama Now," *American Spectator*, vol. I (September 1933) p. 2, and "Perberty in Los Angeles," *American Spectator*, vol. II (Jan. 1934) p. 4.
3. Lillian Hellman, "I Meet the Front Line Russians," *Colliers*, vol. 11 (31 March, 1945) p. 11, 68-69.
4. N. Ephron, "Lillian Hellman Walking, etc." *New York Times Book Review* (23 September, 1972) p. 2.
5. Lillian Hellman, "Sophronia's Grandson Goes to Washington," *Ladies' Home Journal*, 80 (December, 1963) pp. 78-80.
6. In *Pentimento* the old black woman, Caroline Ducky, remarks of Hellman's mother, "Your Ma's changed. City no good for country folk, your Ma and me."

7. Pentimento

1. Christine Doudna, "A Still Unfinished Woman," *Rolling Stone*, Issue 233 (24 February, 1977) p. 53.

2. Ibid., p. 54.
3. Judith Weinraub, "Two Feisty Feminists Filming Hellman's 'Pentimento'," *New York Times* (31 October, 1976) p. 17.

8. SCOUNDREL TIME

1. John F. Baker, "Lillian Hellman," *Publisher's Weekly*, vol. 209 (26 April, 1976) p. 6.
2. "Being Too Comfortable," *The Economist*, 261 (20 November, 1976) p. 140.
3. Nathan Glazer, "An Answer to Lillian Hellman," *Commentary*, 61 (June, 1976) pp. 36-39.
4. William Phillips, "What Happened in the Fifties," *Partisan Review*, 43, No. 3 (1976) pp. 337-340.
5. *New York Times* (24 September, 1976) pp. 1, 45.
6. Irving Howe, "Lillian Hellman and the McCarthy Years," *Dissent*, (Fall 1976) pp. 378-382.
7. Richard Mayne, "Ishmael and the Inquisitors," *Times Literary Supplement*, 12 November 1976, p. 1413. Letters from Diana Trilling and others, 3 December, p. 1516; 10 December, 1560; 17 December, p. 1586.
8. William F. Buckley, Jr., "Who is the Ugliest of them All?" *National Review*, 29 (21 January, 1977) pp. 101-106.
9. Alfred Kazin, "The Legend of Lillian Hellman," *Esquire*, 88 (August, 1977) pp. 28, 30, 34.
10. "Who's Who" Edition I, Show 9, March 8, 1977.
11. Sidney Hook, "Lillian Hellman's Scoundrel Time," *Encounter*, vol. 48 (February, 1977) pp. 82-91.
12. Diana Trilling, *We Must March My Darlings*, (New York and London: Harcourt, Brace, Jovanovich, 1977) 45-50.
13. Thomas R. Edwards, "A Provocative Moral Voice," *The New York Times Book Review* (29 May, 1977) p. 17.
14. Richard A. Falk, "*Scoundrel Time*: Mobilizing the Intelligentsia for the Cold War" *Performing Arts Journal*, vol. 1 (Winter, 1977) pp. 97-102.

Richard Gillam, "Intellectuals and Power," *The Center Magazine*, vol. 10 (May/June, 1977) pp. 27-28.

15. Lev Kopelev, *To Be Preserved Forever* (Philadelphia and New York: J. B. Lippincott Company, 1977) pp. 260-261.

16. Ibid. "Foreword" (unpaginated).

Bibliography

WORKS BY LILLIAN HELLMAN

1. Books

The Collected Plays. Boston-Toronto: Little, Brown and Co., 1972. The definitive text of the plays. Contents: "The Children's Hour," "Days to Come," "The Little Foxes," "Watch on the Rhine," "The Searching Wind," "Another Part of the Forest," "Montserrat," "The Autumn Garden," "The Lark," "Candide," "Toys in the Attic," "My Mother, My Father, and Me."

Four Plays. New York: Random House, 1942. Contents: Introduction by Lillian Hellman, "The Children's Hour," "Days to Come," "The Little Foxes," and "Watch on the Rhine."

Six Plays. New York: Random House, 1960. Contents: Introduction by Lillian Hellman, "Another Part of the Forest," "The Autumn Garden," "The Children's Hour," "Days to Come," "The Little Foxes," and "Watch on the Rhine."

The Children's Hour. New York: Knopf, 1934 and London: Hamish Hamilton, 1937.

Days to Come. New York and London: Knopf, 1936.

The Little Foxes. New York: Random House, and London: Hamish Hamilton, 1939.

Watch on the Rhine. New York: Random House, 1941, and London: English Theatre Guild, 1946.

The Searching Wind. New York: Viking Press, 1944.

Another Part of the Forest. New York: Viking Press, 1947.

Montserrat, adaptation of a play by Emmanuel Roblès. New York: Dramatists Play Service, 1950.

The Autumn Garden. Boston: Little, Brown and Co., 1951.

The Lark, adaptation of a play by Jean Anouilh. New York: Random House, 1955.

Candide, music by Leonard Bernstein, lyrics by Richard Wilbur, John LaTouche, and Dorothy Parker, adaptation of the novel by Voltaire. New York: Random House, 1957.

Toys in the Attic. New York: Random House, 1960.

My Mother, My Father and Me, adaptation of the novel *How Much?* by Burt Blechman. New York: Random House, 1963.

The North Star: A Motion Picture about Some Russian People. New York: Viking Press, 1943.

An Unfinished Woman: A Memoir. Boston-Toronto: Little, Brown and Co., 1969.

Pentimento: A Book of Portraits. Boston-Toronto: Little, Brown and Co., 1973.

Scoundrel Time with introduction by Garry Wills. Boston-Toronto: Little Brown and Co., 1976. English edition, Introduction by James Cameron, Commentary by Garry Wills. London: Macmillan, 1976.

The Letters of Anton Chekhov, edited and with an introduction by Lillian Hellman. Translated by Sidonie Lederer. New York: Farrar, Straus, 1955.

The Big Knockover: Stories and Short Novels by Dashiell Hammett. Introduction by Lillian Hellman. New York: Random House, 1966. As *The Dashiell Hammett Story Omnibus*. London: Cassell, 1966.

2. *Articles*

"Author Jabs the Critic." *New York Times* (15 December 1946) 2, p. 3.

"Back of those Foxes." *New York Times* (26 February 1939) 10, p. 1.

"A Day in Spain." *New Republic*, 94 (13 April 1938) p. 140.

"I Call Her Mama Now." *American Spectator*, I (September 1933) p. 2.

"I Meet the Front Line Russians." *Colliers*, 11 (31 March 1945) pp. 11, 68-69.

"Interlude in Budapest." *Holiday*, 42 (November 1967) pp. 60-61.

"The Land that Holds the Legend of our Lives." *Ladies' Home Journal* 81 (April 1964) pp. 56-7, 122-24.

"Perberty in Los Angeles." *American Spectator*, II (January 1934) p. 4.

"Reports on Yugoslavia." *New York Star* (4 November, p. 13; 5 November, p. 9; 7 November, p. 8; 8 November, p. 1, 9; 9 November, p. 6; 10 November, p. 11, 1948).

"Scotch on the Rocks." *The New York Review of Books*, 1 (17 October 1963) p. 6.

"Sophronia's Grandson Goes to Washington." *Ladies' Home Journal*, 80 (December 1963) pp. 78-80.

"Plain Speaking with Mrs. Carter." *Rolling Stone* (18 November 1976) pp. 43-45.

"The Time of the Foxes." *New York Times* (22 October 1967) 2, p. 1.

WORKS ABOUT LILLIAN HELLMAN

1. Books

Adler, Jacob H. *Lillian Hellman*. Southern Writers Series No. 4. Austin, Texas: Steck-Vaughn Co., 1969.

Holmin, Lorena Ross. *The Dramatic Works of Lillian Hellman*. Uppsala: Almqvist & Wiksell, 1973.

Moody, Richard. *Lillian Hellman, Playwright*. New York: Pegasus, 1972.

Triesch, Manfred. *The Lillian Hellman Collection at the University of Texas*. Austin: The University of Texas Press, 1966. Descriptive bibliography.

2. Other Critical and Biographical Writings

Adler, Jacob H. "Miss Hellman's Two Sisters." *Educational Theatre Journal*, 15 (May 1963) pp. 110-117.

Atkinson, Brooks. "The Play: *The Children's Hour*." *New York Times* (21 November 1934) p. 23.

Baker, John F. "Lillian Hellman." *Publisher's Weekly*, 209 (26 April 1976) pp. 6-7.

Bentley, Eric. "Lillian Hellman's Indignation." *The Dramatic Event: An American Chronicle*. New York: Horizon Press, 1953.

———— (ed.) *Thirty Years of Treason, Excerpts from Hearings before the House Committee on Un-American Activities, 1938-1968*. New York: The Viking Press, 1971.

Buckley, William F., Jr. "Who is the Ugliest of them All?" *National Review*, 29 (21 January 1977) pp. 101-106.

Downer, Alan S. *Recent American Drama*. Minneapolis: University of Minnesota Press, 1961.

Doudna, Christine. "A Still Unfinished Woman." *Rolling Stone* (24 February 1977) pp. 53-56.

Edwards, Thomas R. "A Provocative Moral Voice." *The New York Times Book Review* (29 May 1977) pp. 1, 17.

Ephron, Nora. "Lillian Hellman Walking, Cooking, Writing, Talking." *The New York Times Book Review* (23 September 1973) pp. 2, 51.

Falk, Richard A. "*Scoundrel Time*: Mobilizing the Intelligentsia for the Cold War." *Performing Arts Journal*, 1 (Winter 1977) pp. 97-102.

Feldheim, Marvin. "*The Autumn Garden*: Mechanics and Dialectics." *Modern Drama*, 3 (September 1960) pp. 191-195.

Gassner, John. *Theatre at the Crossroads*. New York: Holt, Rinehart, Winston, 1960.

Glazer, Nathan. "An Answer to Lillian Hellman." *Commentary*, 61 (June 1976) pp. 36-39.

Goldstein, Malcolm. *The Political Stage: American Drama and Theater in the Great Depression*. New York: Oxford University Press, 1974.

Harriman, Margaret Case. "Miss Lily of New Orleans: Lillian Hellman." *Take Them Up Tenderly*. New York: Alfred A. Knopf, 1945.

Howe, Irving. "Lillian Hellman and the McCarthy Years." *Dissent* (Fall 1976) pp. 378-382.

Kazin, Alfred. "The Legend of Lillian Hellman." *Esquire*, 88 (August 1977) pp. 28, 30, 34.

Mantle, Burns (ed). *The Best Plays of 1934-35*. New York: Dodd, Mead and Co., 1935. (Other volumes appropriate to dates of Hellman's plays are also useful and are cited in footnotes.)

Meehan, Thomas. "Q: Miss Hellman, What's Wrong with Broadway? A: It's a Bore." *Esquire*, 58 (December 1962) pp. 140, 142, 235-236.

Moyers, Bill. "Lillian Hellman; The Great Playwright Candidly Reflects on a Long, Rich Life," The Center for Cassette Studies 36648-1974.

Phillips, John and Hollander, Anne. "Lillian Hellman" in *Writers at Work: The Paris Review Interviews*, Third Series. Introduction by Alfred Kazin. New York: The Viking Press, 1967.

Phillips, William. "What Happened in the Fifties." *Partisan Review*, 43 (1976) pp. 337-340.

Poirier, Richard. "*Pentimento: A Book of Portraits* by Lillian Hellman." *The Washington Post* Book Review Section (16 September 1973) pp. 1, 4, 5.

Reed, Rex. *Valentines and Vitriol*. New York: Delacorte Press, 1977.

Sievers, W. David. *Freud on Broadway*. New York: Hermitage House, 1955.

Smiley, Sam. *The Drama of Attack*. Columbia: University of Missouri Press, 1972.

Stern, Richard G. "Lillian Hellman on her Plays." *Contact*, 3 (1959) pp. 113-119.

Trilling, Diana. *We Must March my Darlings*. New York and London: Harcourt, Brace, Jovanovich, 1977.

Weales, Gerald. *American Drama Since World War II*. New York: Harcourt, Brace and World, Inc., 1962.

Weinraub, Judith. "Two Feisty Feminists Filming Hellman's 'Pentimento.'" *New York Times* (31 October 1976) p. 17.

Index

MODERN LITERATURE MONOGRAPHS

In the same series (continued from page ii)